GROWING
from
SEED

Karen Platt
Compiler of the Seed Search

Published by Karen Platt

www.seedsearch.demon.co.uk

To my one seed may he grow and grow.

British Library Cataloguing in publication data.
A catalogue record of this book is available in the British Library.

ISBN 0 9528810 4 7

Written, edited, typeset and illustrated by:
Karen Platt
35 Longfield Rd
Crookes
Sheffield
S10 1QW
www.seedsearch.demon.co.uk

Cover design:
Alan Coventry
Sheffield
www.ac-design.demon.co.uk

CONTENTS

INTRODUCTION

WHY GROW FROM SEED?

There are so many plants available at nurseries, garden centres and even supermarkets. More plants are sold as plugs each year and they look so tantalising in glossy brochures to tempt you. So, why bother growing from seed, and isn't it just for gardeners with real skill and a glasshouse? Time and time again, I am confronted with this idea that growing from seed is difficult and if you try you will fail. Think again.

In this book I aim to show you that it is not difficult to grow most species from seed. True, there are a few species which present a real challenge, but there are thousands which are easy to grow from seed. For those of you who, like me, do not have a glasshouse, you can still grow the vast majority of annuals, biennials and perennials as well as shrubs, climbers, trees, herbs and vegetables. Even tender species can be attempted with the aid of an airing cupboard and a light, bright windowsill. There are also seeds which children can grow very easily. So many species can be sown direct outdoors including herbs and vegetables.

There are three reasons why I recommend that you grow from seed. The main reason is the satisfaction it gives you. There is nothing like the reward of seeing your own little seed pot sprouting like cress. This amazing feeling never diminishes, no matter how often you see it happen. It is something akin to magic. You put seeds in contact with compost, give them the right conditions, and anything from a couple of days onwards, depending on what you have sown, hey presto, the seedlings push their way out of the soil.

As if this is not enough, anyone who is really interested in growing from seed and obtains a copy of The Seed Search will be overwhelmed by the number of seeds available - there are an amazing 43,000 seeds which are available out there, and new ones are being introduced each year. Now when did you last see over 40,000 species of plants for sale in a garden centre or nursery, or that many plugs on offer? With seed we have a much wider choice. The Seed Search is available direct, the address is given on the inside back cover.

In addition, there is the economy aspect, why pay so much for a few plugs or a single plant, when you can buy a packet of seed for much less and sow many more plants? Your garden can be teeming with colour and interesting plants. It does not matter if it is not commercially viable, if it pleases you and you can obtain the seed, you can grow it. If you do not need many plants of one species, seal the packet carefully, most seeds can be stored and if done so correctly will last from one to many years depending on the species. Or look at it as a bonus, not only have you made your garden the most colourful in the street, but you have enough plants to give to friends and family, they will be amazed that you grew them all yourself.

You do not even need a garden, choose seed suitable for window boxes and containers or hanging baskets, including herbs and vegetables. Do you need any more persuasion to try this fascinating aspect of gardening?

The great plant hunters sent seed to nurseries to raise species new to us. Seeds came from far afield including China and the Himalaya. Seed still remains the way to raise most species which are rarely available as plants, and of course annuals must be raised from seed each year and it is the natural way to raise the tastiest vegetables.

I am often told by quite avid gardeners that they do not grow from seed because it is too difficult or they do not have a greenhouse. I would like to dispel this myth. I have concentrated here on providing you with the necessary information to germinate seed easily. There is a specific table on genera which is easy from seed and many of the seeds can be sown direct or indoors with little heat to demonstrate just how many species can be sown easily without any special knowledge, exceptional green fingers or expensive equipment. Seed is not difficult, most species are easily raised from seed, and many more with a little pre-treatment become easy, leaving only a few difficult species for the person who wants a real challenge. You can raise seed with very little equipment and a greenhouse is not a requirement, it is an extra, if you have one you can attempt more tender species. Even so, these can be germinated in an airing cupboard and raised with success indoors. You do not even need purpose made pots, you can use old yoghurt pots that have been disinfected and scrubbed clean and pierced for drainage holes.

If it is your first attempt or you have had failures in the past start with something easy and build up to more challenging subjects. There are many seeds that are so easy, it is almost impossible to fail. Give any seed the right conditions to thrive and it will reward you by doing just that.

My aim is to give you the confidence to grow from seed with ease. So, join me in growing from seed and you can reap the rewards.

Karen Platt 1999

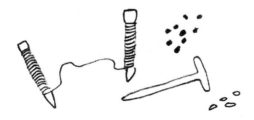

HOW TO USE THIS BOOK

This book is intended to help you grow from seed. It has been designed so that you can choose species suitable to grow under the conditions you are able to provide. It explains everything you need to know, listing concise details on all aspects of growing from seed and practical techniques on sowing seed and aftercare. In addition it explains the process of pollination, seed development, germination to provide greater understanding of how seed is formed and how it germinates. There are also fascinating aspects of seed growing included such as collecting and storing seed, viability, edible seeds, medicinal uses and a did you know section.

There are detailed tables which are arranged according to plant type. Short-lived or tender perennials which are grown by many as annuals, such as Pelargonium are classified under perennials. The tables begin with annuals and biennials and all other plant types are classified under other genera. They are classified by headings so that you can see at a glance where to sow, i.e. direct or under cover. You can also immediately see if heat is required or not as the headings specify cold in spring or cold in autumn making it easy for the gardener without a greenhouse to see that many genera can still be raised outdoors. Vegetables have their own tables being classified under two headings of sowing direct and sowing under cover. Where a particular species has different requirements in general to the rest of the genus, they are given for that species. Where a particular genus includes both annuals and perennials if the method is the same, they have only been listed under one heading and you can assume the same treatment is required.

The tables are designed to show the requirements needed to germinate seed of the genus. If a particular temperature is required then it is given after the genus, I have normally stated the minimum temperature, followed by any other requirements which will aid germination. A particular genus may have more than one entry, for example those annuals which can be sown under cover in early spring and sown outdoors in mid-late spring may be found under both appropiate sections of the book. The tables are in A-Z format throughout and are easy to use.

General techniques are explained for all plant types. Here you will find average temperatures and the best type of compost to use amongst other useful information. Tips are also found throughout giving additional information to make seed sowing easier.

I have used Botanical names throughout with the exception of the Vegetable and Herb sections, where common names are usually the norm. For common names and synonyms of plant names as well as an explanation of latin terms you can do no better than check out Plant Names A-Z, it is available direct, see the inside back cover.

ABBREVIATIONS

The following abbreviations have been used throughout the tables in the book.

alp alpines
an annual
au autumn
B immerse seed in boiling water for 20 seconds
BH bottom heat
bi biennial
** can also be sown in autumn
* can also be sown in spring
CF cold frame
CG expose to winter cold until germination, then transfer to a cold greenhouse
CH chip
CL cloche protection
CS clean seed
D germinate in complete darkness
DC damp compost
DE doubly dormant
DP deep pots
e early (as in e-sr early spring)
EC expose to cold
EF expose to frost
ER ericaceous compost (lime-free)
^ erratic or slow to germinate
EX expose to light
F fresh seed
FF flowers first year (per /bi)
fr-H frost hardy
FT needs fluctating temperatures of -2°C (28°F) at night, 10°C (50°F) in the day.
H hardy
H spp hardy species
HA hardy annual
HH half hardy
KF keep pots frost free for the first year
KS keep shaded in summer
l late (as in l-sr late spring)
LU leave undisturbed
m mid (as in m-sr mid-spring)

MC very moist compost
MO module
MS partly submerged in water
N notes under did you know section
NZ New Zealand
OF open frame
PC moist pre-chill at 0-1°C (32-34°F)
per perennial
PG equal parts of peat, grit and loam
PS permanently damp compost in shade
R remove flesh from seed
R ripe
SC scarify
SD sow direct
SG sow when still slightly green
SH place in shade
SI singly
SM sow on damp sphagnum moss
sm spp small species
SO soak
spp species
sr spring
SS surface sow
ST stratify
SU sow in succession
su summer
succ succulents
T dislikes root disturbance
TH sow thinly
UG under glass
VG very gritty compost
VS very sandy compost
VT very thinly, leave in pot
WB water from below
WF whole fruit
wi winter
WS scatter seed on surface of water as soon as ripe
WT stand the pot in a tray of water

WHY DO SEEDS FAIL?

Look in the small print of seed catalogues and you will find that they nearly always say that they accept no responsibility for the failure of seeds to germinate. Why does one seed germinate and another fail?

FRESH SEED

If you are not collecting your own seed from plants in the garden or exchanging seed with friends, it can be difficult to obtain fresh seed. Fresh seed should be sought above all else, it will always germinate freely. The only other alternative is to buy seed which has been stored.

Most commercial seed suppliers store seed cold. If you are storing seed at home, keep it in a dry place at a temperature of 3-5°C. Never store seed in a hot place or in a damp, humid place, its viability will deteriorate drastically. Assuming that the seed has been stored correctly, and is still viable, it should germinate reasonably well. Old seed almost never germinates as well as fresh seed, but there are exceptions.

ENSURING SUCCESS

Most seeds fail because they are not stored correctly. Packets are left open or are exposed to high temperatures being left in the greenhouse or on a windowsill. See how to store seeds later in the book.

Other factors largely governing failure to germinate is that the seeds are overwatered or exposed to the wrong temperature. Always use a fine rose, moisten compost sufficiently before sowing and always check the temperature. Seeds dislike wildly fluctuating temperatures. Excessively high temperatures can inhibit germination just as much as low temperatures. Remember in all cases it is the soil temperature that is important and not the air temperature. A propagator is useful, but not absolutely essential, if you intend to raise many seeds which require minimum temperatures above 21°C. Seed packets often give the germination time expected for species, so you can check if the seeds have come up in time. Seed, given the right conditions, can come up from 24 hours onwards. Seeds at lower than usual temperatures will often germinate, but more slowly.

If the soil is compacted or frozen, waterlogged or left to dry out, oxygen cannot reach the seed and it will die.

Too much fertiliser given at germination stage will probably kill the resultant seedlings, seeds need to be raised in a low nutrient compost, they have their own food stores.

One hundred per cent germination is not an every day occurence, it is good when it happens. Be patient, do not throw away your seed pots after a few months, keep them, depending on the species up to 4 years. Plump, healthy seeds will provide the best germination rate, some species do have very poor viability. Given the right conditions, and tender loving care you will have success with growing from seed. Once you get the bug, it is difficult to stop.

SOWING INSTRUCTIONS

GENERAL

Choose the type of compost indicated and a suitable container such as a pot, tray, module into which you wish to sow. All containers and equipment must be scrupulously clean. Remember a tray can hold as many as 1,000 seedlings and it is not unusual to sow 100 seeds into a small pot. It is wise to sow just a few more seeds than you need plants to allow for disappointments.

Fill the pot loosely with compost and strike off any surplus with a piece of wood or board. Firm lightly, you need to remove air pockets, but you do not want compacted compost. I use the bottom of another pot for this purpose. The level of the compost should be 1cm below the rim. Water using a fine rose. If you have been heavy handed and think the pots are too wet, let the pots stand and drain for awhile before sowing your seeds. The compost needs to be adequately moist but not overwet. Never use any compost which is older than six months.

Sowing seed

When sown, cover the seeds with compost to no more than their own depth. Large seeds are easy to handle, space in the pot. Fine seeds tend to be tricky and there are several methods you can use to help. Use a seed sower. You can also put the seeds onto a folded sheet of paper, placing them into the V fold, and tap gently. Both methods are intended to help sow seeds evenly by controlling the flow. Another method is to mix fine seeds with sand. What I prefer to do is to take a pinch of seed and sprinkle carefully. Like most good things, it takes a little practice and you will make mistakes, but it is the best method for me. Fine seeds are usually better surface sown, whereas other larger seeds are better covered with a little compost. If sowing in autumn it is also advisable to use vermiculite as a top dressing.

Place your seeds into the right environment as regards light and temperature and you will be rewarded by the amazing sight of seeds coming up like cress. There is nothing quite like it. Pots do not normally need watering again until seedlings have emerged. Do not let any pots dry out, if they do need watering, use a very fine rose and water gently so as not to disturb the seeds or emerging seedlings. You can water from the bottom, but it is not a method I would normally advocate.

You can use the airing cupboard to raise seeds, but remove as soon as seedlings are beginning to emerge, so do check every day. Trays need to be covered with clingfilm or a lid, these will need removing when the seedlings emerge. The film can be split first, so as not to provide a check in growth. Seeds can also be raised on a windowsill, but do not keep behind closed curtains. You can also invest in purpose-built propagators if you are going to sow a lot of seeds which need a high temperature. Propagators will need to be ventilated when seedlings appear. Ventilate gradually, then remove the lid altogether.

Using modules is useful for seedlings which resent disturbance and also cuts down on the work of pricking out. Large seeds can easily be sown into the compartments of a module tray which come in varying sizes and produce small plug plants which have a good root system.

EQUIPMENT

If sowing direct, you will need general gardening tools such as a fork, rake, spade and hoe. There are a number of special items of equipment for seed sowing. They are usually not essential, but can make life easier. Most of the equipment can be thoroughly cleaned and used again.

Containers

You can buy seed trays of different weights, always buy the sturdiest you can afford, it is more cost-effective in the long run. This is also applicable to pots and other containers such as modules. You do not need to buy containers and can make do with reusable plastic household containers. Shallow pots are often best for seeds, although deep pots or modules are required for tap-rooted species. Pots come in many shapes and sizes, and are made in varying materials, clay is still my preferred material, but I often sow in square plastic pots as they fit better into a tray. Plastic pots retain moisture, but clay pots provide better drainage and aeration.

Labels

This is one item that is indispensable. Forget to label your pots and you will probably never recognise what is in them. This is also applicable to collected seed. Labels come in many shapes and sizes. I use simple white plastic labels most of the time. Mark them with a pencil or buy a label marker.

Other useful equipment for seed-sowing

A seed sower may prove useful. a hand-held type is not expensive. A dibber is handy, but a pencil can work just as well for making planting holes in compost or soil. Use a garden line or the flat edge of a board to give a straight line when sowing seeds direct. Metal sieves are useful if collecting your own seed of fleshy fruits such as berries or tomatoes.

You may find a potting tidy very useful, I use the grass collector from my lawn mower for this purpose. A mist sprayer is useful for seeds which require high humidity. A wooden compost presser is one item I would cross off my list, use the bottom of another pot.

Propagation aids

In cooler climates, protection must be given to raise some species. This can be indoors, in a propagator, in a cloche, coldframe or a greenhouse. A sunny windowsill will help germinate many seeds, do not place in full sun. A propagator provides high humidity and a controlled temperature if it is heated. A cloche can be used to warm the soil, gives protection and thereby extends the growing season. Coldframes provide shelter and can be put to excellent use in hardening off small plants. A greenhouse is a valuable asset if you wish to raise plants. A cool or heated greenhouse will determine the variety of species you can grow. The choice is yours, I find with my limited space, I can grow most species with the aid of cloche, a coldframe and my windowsill.

SOWING DIRECT

There are a large number of seeds which can be sown direct and it is the easiest method for many gardeners. You need no special equipment, just a packet of seeds and well-prepared ground.

The most important preparation is to rid the land of weeds or you will not be able to tell the difference at the early stages between the seedlings and the weeds. In fact, I have an odd theory that weeds can mimic seedlings.

PREPARING THE GROUND

Wait until the soil is workable. Remove all litter and weeds from the area. Firm the ground so that it is free of air pockets. This is best done by shuffling back and forth. Rake the area in all directions to create a fine tilth. If the soil is dry, water thoroughly.

SOWING A BORDER

Bear in mind the sowing space of the species you are going to sow and allow enough room, dividing the area into a grid. You can work in drills or broadcast seed. Use canes and string to help define areas for sowing, or mark lines with sand or grit. Scatter seeds thinly, pelleted or larger seeds can be sown individually.

Drills look formal at first, but soon blend and are easier to recognise from weeds. Use a hoe to draw a line for sowing, or the edge of a long straight piece of wood. Drills should be no more than 2.5cm (1in) deep. Keep them a uniform depth for even germination. Water in well, keep the soil moist and weed-free.

Broadcast seeds can be sown amongst other plants. Weeding is more difficult, but this is the ideal method for filling gaps.

Seedlings will probably need thinning to the required spacings to avoid overcrowding. Do this when the soil is moist and the weather fine. You can thin in several stages if the desired spacing is more than 20cm (8 in) apart. Remove the weakest seedlings.

MARKING OUT A BORDER

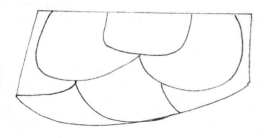

THINNING SEEDLINGS

Strong seedlings can be transplanted to another site to fill gaps. Tap-rooted species such as Papaver, Clarkia, Eschscholzia and Gypsophila do not transplant well. Water in carefully but thoroughly.

VEGETABLES

Purchased seeds are required to meet certain standards, so you can buy with confidence. Unfortunately, varieties have to be registered on the National List, which is quite costly, so you will only find seed offered if it is considered commercially viable. Expensive F1 seed gives uniform plants, perhaps useful to the commercial supplier of vegetables, but of relatively little use to the home gardener who can use open-pollinated varieties to great effect in the garden. Some varieties have inbred disease-resistance.

You can purchase seeds as they come, or those which have been treated in some way. Primed or sprinter seeds are specially treated to germinate quicker than untreated seeds. Primed seed is also larger and easier to sow. Chitted seed is pregerminated and useful for species which are difficult to germinate such as cucumber. Pelleted seeds are coated and easier to handle than normal seed, they require moister conditions. Coated and dusted seeds are treated with fungicide and need to be handled with gloves.

Vegetables can be grown in drills or beds. Some varieties are suitable for growing in containers, grow bags or even hanging baskets and window boxes.

The bed system with paths in between is a popular way of growing vegetables and a raised bed is advantageous as it warms up more quickly in spring. If you dig the soil deeply for a deep-bed system you can plant crops up to four times more closely, thereby greatly increasing the yield. Intercropping also makes good use of even the smallest place. Quick maturing crops such as radish are grown in between rows of slower crops such as cabbages.

Most vegetables prefer a sunny, sheltered site with a free-draining, moisture retentive, slightly acid soil rich in nutrients. Dig over the patch in autumn adding plenty of well-rotted organic matter. You will not be able to sow seed of root crops, with the exception of potatoes on freshly manured ground. In spring loosen up the soil and add a balanced feed.

Before sowing, rake over to a fine tilth. Most vegetables need to be sown at a soil temperature of 7°C (45°F) to germinate. Some tender crops, such as sweetcorn, need higher temperatures, refer to the table. Lettuce will not germinate in high temperatures.

When sowing direct, protect from birds with mesh. Horticultural fleece can be used to extend the growing season. Carrots should not be thinned, this encourages carrot fly. Most other seedlings, unless space-sown, will need thinning as for annuals sown direct. Cabbage, lettuce and onion seedlings can be transplanted, water in well. Experiment, vegetables can even be sown in the border.

BOLTING

Some vegetables have a tendency to bolt. This is usually, though not always, triggered by a cold spell. Once the crop runs to seed the process cannot be halted. Beetroot, carrot, leeks, onions, swedes and turnips often produce flowers after a period of cold. Delay sowings of the above until temperatures are stable. This is particularly advisable for endive, Swiss chard and turnips. Early crops of beetroot, kohlrabi and onion can be raised in modules under cover and planted out in stable temperatures. Keep plants well-watered.

SOWING IN CONTAINERS

If seeds cannot be sown direct, they are normally sown in trays or pots. Different genera need different treatment as you can see below.

ALPINES

For many alpines you will achieve the best results if they are sown when the seed is ripe, otherwise try them in winter or early spring. A hand lens and tweezers will help to ease out seed of cushion alpines that are buried under new leaves.

Many alpines will not germinate until they have received a period of cold stratification. On germination some seedlings will need protection. If older seed has become shrunken or wrinkled, soak before sowing.

Most alpines will be suited with a compost of loam and sharp grit or coarse sand. Acantholimon and Dionysia need double the quantity of sharp grit. Sow thinly and cover all but very fine seed with a very thin layer of compost, topping with a 5-10mm layer of sharp grit. A cold-frame is ideal and some prefer an open frame, a shaded position is best. Watch carefully for erratic germinators, teasing seedlings out and keeping the pot for stragglers for at least 2 years and up to 4 years if possible.

GESNERIADS

These alpines need special treatment because they have dust-like seed. They need to be surface-sown. Try sowing on fresh, finely-chopped moss or on sterilized peat-based seed compost. Cover the container and leave in a cool, shaded place. Water from below if necessary to avoid removing the lid and eliminating as far as possible the risk of disease. The seedlings develop slowly and can be left in the container with the lid in place until their second year.

PERENNIALS

Seeds are often sown in pots, although some that dislike disturbance are better sown in modules or singly. Loam-based seed composts are best for most perennials. Keep pots for at least one year as seeds can germinate erratically.

Sowing too thickly leads to spindly seedlings and damping off. Seeds can be covered with compost or, for those needing light to germinate or germinate quickly, top-dress with vermiculite. Water with a fine rose, cover and shade from sun if necessary. You may wish to place the seeds in a propagator. Remove any cover when the seeds germinate. For most perennials, seeds will germinate well at a temperature of 15.5°C (60°F), and fully frost hardy seeds at 10°C (50°F). Frost tender species need a minimum of 20°C (68°F). They will germinate at lower temperatures, but will take longer. Check with the temperatures given for individual genera in the tables.

Autumn-sown perennials in the cold-frame should be covered with a layer of fine gravel or coarse sand. They can be left in an open frame or a plunge bed. Pots can be covered with a fine mesh to protect from birds or mice.

ANNUALS AND BIENNIALS

Pots, pans, seed trays and modular trays are suitable. Choose the correct container for the amount of seed you wish to sow. Seeds can be sown straight from the packet. Fine seeds can be sown with sand and need no extra covering. Other seeds need a layer of compost or vermiculite. Cover trays with clingfilm, a sheet of glass or plastic, or a propagator lid. Shade from direct sun if necessary.

Temperatures vary according to genus, so check with the tables given. Seeds can be easily raised on a windowsill in a warm room. Remove the cover as soon as germination occurs. Place the container in full light, shading from strong sun. Keep the compost moist at all times. Seed can also be sown direct.

BROMELIADS

When seed can be obtained (rare in cultivation) these are rewarding subjects to grow from seed. Tillandsias readily set seed, but many other Bromeliads are self-sterile unless two or more of the same species are grown. Hand-pollination can help to set seeds in cultivation. The seeds are only viable for a maximum of a month or two, or a few weeks for plumed seed.

Use a fine sterilized seed compost or orchid compost. Scatter seeds thinly over the surface, leaving seeds from berries on the surface, but covering winged or plumed seeds with a fine layer of coarse grit. Cover with glass to retain humidity and sheets of polystyrene to retain warmth and give shade. The minimum temperature for germination is 19-27°C (66-81°F).

Epiphytic bromeliads can be scattered onto a bundle of twigs, such as those from a conifer which have been tied into a bundle with a little moist sphagnum moss. If they do not adhere, tie in with raffia. They can be misted lightly with a sprayer and hung in a shaded warm place with 100 per cent humidity, such as a propagator or mist propagation bench. Keep moist by spraying regularly, or daily submerge in clean rainwater.

TREES

Generally a straightforward and inexpensive process. Seedlings establish well and are usually virus-free. Seedlings take longer than cuttings of course, maybe 2-5 times longer, and can vary in appearance, hardiness and growth. They are usually better from fresh seed, but if stored correctly will germinate well. Pre-treatment before sowing is important especially for species from northern temperate regions. Seeds may need to have wings, husks etc, removed.

Seeds can be sown in pots which gives you more control than direct sowing. Use deep pots or root trainers for tap-rooted species such as Quercus and Eucalyptus. Seed can also be sown direct.

A free-draining, mildly acid, soilless compost is best. For lime-hating trees such as Arbutus, use an ericaceous compost. Seeds which take more than 12 months to germinate are better sown in a heavier, loam-based compost. Cover with fine grit or small gravel, or for quick germinators, use vermiculite. Pots should be placed in a sheltered spot at the temperature given in the tables. A minimum night temperature of 10°C (50°F) is required and tender species will require 15-20°C (59-68°F). Always keep pots until at least the second spring.

BULBOUS PLANTS

A rewarding if slow task. Rare species are often only available as seed, and woodland species are often best from fresh seed. Seed is always disease-free so is a good way of propagating plants which easily succumb to virus such as Lilium. Ripe capsules are often brown and soon shed their seed.

Freshly sown seed is most succesful providing even germination in the following spring. Seeds will normally remain viable for a year if kept cool. In cool climates, frost and severe winters may prevent the fresh sowing of seed.

Sow in 9cm deep pots for quickly formed storage organs. Equal parts of loam-based compost and fine grit or coarse sand is suitable for sowing in clay pots. For lime-hating species, mix equal parts of peat or coir and fine lime-free grit. With plastic pots use six parts grit to four of compost to avoid waterlogging. Cover the seeds with compost and top-dress with fine grit.

A winter freeze for hardy species, and frost-free chill for half-hardy species, and a thaw at 10°C (50°F) often aids germination. Tender seeds need a frost-free environment, see the tables. Wet seeds will rot, dry seeds will die. Autumn sowings are often more sussessful than spring sowings for most species. A plunge bed provides the best environment, with seeds sown in clay pots. Pots can also be kept in a cool, shady area such as a cold frame. Some species germinate rapidly but most autumn-sown seeds will appear in the first mild spell of late winter. Most seedlings will have grass-like leaves. Some bulbous plants such as Paris stay dormant for a year, some Lilium species germinate but do not show their leaves until the following spring, and Arisaemas and Colchicum may germinate erratically for 4 years.

CACTI AND SUCCULENTS

These can be slow-growing but relatively easy from seed. Fresh seed usually gives the best results. Most can be sown in late winter and with warmth will germinate easily. Pediocactus need a period of chilling at 3°C (37°F) for two to four weeks. Unlike most Cactus, Opuntias have large seeds with a thick coat and are not easy to germinate, they may take up to two years.

Collect seed when ripe and sow in small containers. A 5cm (2in) pot is ideal for 25-30 seeds. You can use a specialist cactus compost or mix your own with one part very fine sharp grit or coarse sand and two parts potting compost, sterliized soil or peat. Cover with a shallow layer of grit. Put in a warm position, shaded from direct sun. A propagator is ideal as a temperature of 21-30°C (70-85°F) is necessary, see individual temperatures in the table. Seeds will germinate in 2-3 weeks, taking longer at cooler temperatures, and very poor germination being obtained in temperatures over 32°C (90°F).

CYCADS

Expect a success rate of no more than 50%. A mature male and female cycad is needed to obtain viable seed. The outer woody casing has to be removed as it inhibits germination. Make a shallow cut at one end in the seed coat of viable seed or file. If the seeds are more than two weeks old in warm climates, soak before sowing for 24 hours, and up to 3 days in cooler climates.

A good seed compost is made from equal parts of peat-free compost, for example coir, and three parts coarse grit. Sow singly in deep pots as they are tap-rooted. Leave the seeds half exposed and keep well-watered and misted.

A minimum temperature of 21-30°C (70-86°F) is required for germination and 60-70% relative humidity. In cooler climates you will need a heated propagator or mist unit to provide these conditions. Seeds usually take from four to fifteen months to germinate, fresh seeds being marginally quicker.

PALMS

Palms have fruits with moist or dry flesh. Seeds can be collected when the fruits ripen and change colour. Pulp must be cleaned off to prevent rot and seeds can then be wrapped in damp tissue or peat moss. Dry flesh can be removed by soaking fruits in hot water for 1-2 days. The seeds are best sown fresh, but remain viable for 4-8 weeks if stored damp. Dry, purchased seed needs to be soaked at least 24 hours before sowing. Woody seeds can be filed.

Fill clay pots with a mix of equal parts coir and fine grit. An air temperature of 30-35°C (86-97°F) and high humidity are essential for good germination. Seeds must never be allowed to dry out. Germination can take from three weeks to eighteen months and one would expect about two-thirds of the seed to germinate. Shade well. In cool climates place in a heated propagator with bottom heat of 25-28°C (77-82°F) and place in a greenhouse to provide maximum light and warmth. Mist regularly and ventilate. For large palm seeds such as Lodoicea sow direct in a deep container and leave the seed half exposed.

ROSES

Rose seed can take up to two seasons to germinate. Collect in late summer and store at 21°C (70°F) in a plastic bag in moist coir or peat, vermiculite or sand. Seeds need to be stratified for 2-4 weeks in the top shelf of the refrigerator either as entire hips or extracted seed.

Sow into modules and leave in a coldframe, or other cool, sheltered situation. They may take a year to germinate.

SHRUBS AND CLIMBERS

Choose only healthy plants as seeds can harbour viruses. Some seeds will need pre-treatment, some will be best sown in autumn others in spring, so refer to the table before sowing.

Use a good quality, gritty compost. Most seeds can be covered with a fine layer of compost, top with a layer of fine grit or coarse sand. Spring sowings are better with a layer of vermiculite instead of grit. Tiny seeds need to be surface-sown.

Autumn-sown seeds can overwinter in a sheltered place. They can germinate and remain in their pots in a coldframe up to one year after germination has taken place. They may germinate in the first spring or up to one year later.

Spring-sown seeds often need tempeatures akin to bedding plants and can be raised in a propagator, some will require bottom heat.

VEGETABLES

Sowing in a small pot will provide sufficient vegetables for most needs. Cover the pot with a plastic bag or place in a propagator, ventilating daily to remove excess condensation. Seed is often sown two or three to a pot and the weakest seedlings removed. Vegetables can also be sown in modules, thereby eliminating the need for transplanting, and is essential for plants which dislike root disturbance.

Most vegetables can also be grown successfully in containers, either outdoors or in a glasshouse. Crops such as beans and courgettes can be started indoors and then put outside when the temperature is suitable. Choose large pots with good drainage and you can enjoy fresh vegetables in the tiniest of gardens. Look out for mini or baby vegetables which are excellent for container growing. Grow a variety not available in your supermarket or exotic vegetables that cannot be found locally.

HERBS

Sow into small pots or modules for herbs which dislike disturbance. Do not overwater. Scatter small seed on the surface and cover with a fine layer of vermiculite. Press medium-sized seed into the surface of the compost, cover with their own depth of compost. Space larger seed into the pot, again cover with compost to its own depth. Some herbs will need a period of stratification, especially old seed. Herbs can also be sown direct. The main sowing times for herbs are spring and autumn. Rosemary needs a high temperature and develops rather slowly from seed.

NEED LIGHT TO GERMINATE

The following seed will germinate much better in light. Surface-sow and do not cover with compost. You can still top-dress with vermiculite.

Angelica
Begonia
Bracteantha
Brachyscome
Browallia
Campanula medium
Celery
Chamamaelum
Cynoglossum
Digitalis
Ferraria bright
Impatiens
Ipomoea bright
Leucocoryne
Lobelia
Nicotiana
Origanum majorana
Papaver
Petunia

Primula
Sarracenia
Satureja
Solenostemon
Thymus
Verbena some
Veronica

SOWING TIP

Fine seeds are always surface-sown and do not need to be covered with compost. They usually need light to germinate. Top-dress with vermiculite or perlite. If you find dust-like seeds difficult to sow, tap into the pot from a V-fold in a piece of folded paper.

PRE-SOWING TREATMENTS

Some seeds which have received a reputation for being difficult, need no more than a simple pre-treatment before sowing. None of these techniques are difficult and some are not absolutely vital. Most seeds will still germinate without pre-treatments given time, but these are a way of speeding things up.

SMOKE

Some seed, especially Australian and South African species are exposed to fire in their natural habitat, the fire scarifies and the smoke triggers germination. Place seeds in a terracotta pot and cover with straw or dry bracken. Set alight and water in the ash. Kits can be bought to treat seeds. The hairs on Proteas need to be burned off before they will germinate.

SCARIFYING

Also known as nicking seed or chipping. The idea is to help water penetrate hard or thick seed coats.This method is normally used with hard seed such as that of Lupinus. Chip one end of the seed with a sharp knife. Care must be taken not to damage the eye of the seed or the seed itself, chip at the opposite end removing only a small part of the coat.

This is a laborious task if you have many seeds to chip, and a difficult task with small seed. Wrap sandpaper round the inside of an empty glass jar, put the seeds inside, screw the top on tightly and shake the contents vigorously. In this way the sandpaper will abrase the seeds.

SOAKING

Another method for use with hard seed coats in order to soften them. Also useful for seeds with a water repellent covering such as Fremontodendron and for seeds with germination inhibitors such as Beetroot. Use hot not boiling water and soak for 24 hours. You can use a vacuum flask. Some seeds need soaking for longer or shorter periods, refer to the table.

COLD STRATIFICATION

This is a method of subjecting seeds to a change in temperature. This can be effected by sowing in a cold frame in autumn and letting the naturally cooler temperatures of winter work their magic. Alternatively, you can sow your seeds as usual, cover and place in the refrigerator, thereby mimicking winter weather and tricking the seeds into thinking they have gone through winter. This method is useful for breaking the dormancy of some alpines and hardy trees as well as shrubs.

Some species will only need 3-4 weeks of this treatment, others much longer. Seeds can germinate in the refrigerator, so check them carefully every day and remove as soon as they appear.

WARM STRATIFICATION

Some species, such as Ilex, have seed whose embryo is not fully developed even when the seed is ripe. They cannot germinate until the embryo is further developed. Seed will normally respond to a temperature of 20°C for 60 days during the first summer after the seed was dispersed.

Fraxinus excelsior and Paeonia species have a double dormancy and after receiving the above treatment will need a period of artificial chilling at 1-2°C (34-36°F) for 8-20 weeks to allow them to germinate in the following spring.

AFTERCARE

Seedlings develop seed leaves first, then true leaves typical of the species will come. When the seedlings have two to four true leaves or as soon as they are large enough to handle, prick out into trays or pot up individually. Seedlings left too long will become overcrowded and leggy whilst competing with one another for light. Roots will also become matted and entangled making pricking out more difficult. Always hold seedlings by their leaves and never by the stems. A damaged stem will kill a seedling. Allow seedlings to fill their new pots with roots before planting out. Compost contains enough food for about 4-6 weeks, from then on liquid feed plants regularly or use a season-long feed for containers.

Seedlings raised indoors or under cover need to hardened off before planting out. To harden off, plants can be left outside for longer periods every day to gradually become acclimatized to the change in temperature. Do not expose to full sun at this stage, but harden in a shady spot. Extend the time over a three week period until the plants have been outside all day and night for at least four days, they can then be planted out into their final planting positions. If you have a cold frame, it is an excellent way of hardening plants off, raise the lid gradually until it is fully open even at night.

Once planted out, if frost threatens, cover with horticultural fleece or sheets of newspaper.

Remember that many seeds sown under cover in early spring, can also be sown direct outdoors as soon as the soil temperature is warm enough. This eliminates the need for tasks such as cleaning pots and the aftercare methods of pricking out or potting on and the need for hardening off. Warm the soil beforehand by using cloches or plastic sheeting.

SOWING TIP

Do not sow too thickly as this encourages fungal diseases. Many seedlings die each year from damping off disease. You will know when it strikes, seedlings suddenly go over. The water and soil-borne fungus spreads rapidly in wet compost. There is no treatment at this stage. Some seedlings are very susceptible. Treat with copper fungicide when sowing.

COMPOST

The type of compost you use to raise seeds is important. Above all never use ordinary, unsterilized garden soil.

WHY IS GARDEN SOIL UNSUITABLE?

Simply because it is not sterile. It may contain pathogens and weed seed which will not give the seedlings a fair start. To sterilize garden soil: first sieve to provide a soil without lumps or stones. Heat to a minimum of 200°C (400°F), Gas mark 6, for 30 minutes. A tray of soil can be placed in the oven or you can place the soil in a pierced, sealed roasting bag and place in the microwave on full heat for ten minutes. Special soil-sterilizing units are available.

IS THERE A SPECIAL COMPOST FOR SEEDS?

Yes, there are special seed composts. Normally these will be relatively free-draining and low in nutrients, which are unnecessary at the germination stage. There are also special composts for Cactus and Alpines which need a very free-draining soil and if you are using a normal seed compost, add extra grit for drainage.

Purpose-made seed compost is moisture-retentive so you will probably not have to water again until seedlings emerge. It is fine textured to enable seeds to be able to push through the compost on emergence. You can obtain soilless seed compost, or mixtures of loam, peat (or peat substitute) and sand.

CAN YOU MAKE YOUR OWN COMPOST?

Yes, there is no reason why you should not, and you can mix a compost to suit the needs of the seeds you are sowing.

Ingredients which can be used in composts.

Loam

High-quality sterilized garden compost, with good nutrient supply, drainage, aeration and moisture retention. Used in soil-based composts.

Peat

Stable, well-aerated and moisture retentive, but low in nutrients. Hard to re-wet once dry as water runs off the surface. Lightweight.

Leaf mould

Well-rotted, sieved leaves. Not normally used for seeds.

Coir

Fibrous, retains moisture better than peat, used as a peat-substitute. Excellent base for soilless composts.

Fine bark

Used as a peat substitute. Very free-draining, acidic. Used with orchids and palms.

Grit

Used to improve drainage, especially for Cactus and Alpines.

Sand

Fine, silver sand helps drainage and aeration in seed composts, coarse sand is used for cuttings. Always use horticultural sand.

Vermiculite

Expanded and air-blown mica, holds more water than perlite and less air. Fine grade aids drainage and aeration. Can be mixed into the compost and used as a top dressing.

Perlite

Expanded volcanic rock granules. Sterile and light substance which retains moisture but drains freely therefore improving aeration and drainage. This is not a substance I use, it creates a lot of dust and is definitely unsuitable for asthmatics. Damping down before use might help.

MAKING YOUR OWN COMPOST

Loam-based seed compost

2 parts loam
1 part peat-substitute (or peat)
1 part sand
To each 36 litres (8 gallons) add
42 g superphosphate and 21 g chalk

Ericaceous compost

Add an acid loam and omit the chalk

Soilless seed compost

3 parts peat substitute
1 part fine bark
1 part perlite
To each 36 litres (8 gallons) add
36g slow-release fertilizer and
36g of magnesium limestone
(dolomite)

HOW TO MIX

Observe strict hygiene. All benches where compost is mixed should be sterile, otherwise you could introduce bacteria and minute pests into your compost. Make sure all ingredients are thoroughly mixed. Never compact the compost.

Remember it does not last forever. Compost should be used within six months to keep it sweet. If not used immediately, store in sealed plastic bags to avoid the risk of contamination. Label the bag with the date it was made and discard old, unused compost.

OTHER MEDIUMS

You can also sow seeds direct into inert fibres such as rockwool which is recommended for seeds which dislike disturbance. Seeds are not exposed to pathogens and have access to water, to which nutrients are added and they also have a constant supply of oxygen, the plant's roots are in contact with the air. Rockwool is used by commercial propagators. Compressed peat blocks are also useful for seeds whose roots dislike disturbance. They swell to form individual planting modules once soaked in water. Do not allow to dry out.

There are other peat substitutes such as pine bark, animal waste products such as worm casts or straw which have been composted and heat-treated.

SOWING ANNUALS DIRECT

A large number of annuals can be sown direct in spring, and many also in autumn for early flowers in the following spring, or as pot plants indoors. Some will need protection if sown late. Sow in succession for long-lasting colour. Fill gaps or whole borders. Use the table to show you what to sow.

Adonis
Agrostemma e-sr
Agrostis m-sr
Aira
Althaea
Amaranthus caudatus m-sr
Amberboa ** CL
Ammi **
Anethum graveolens l-sr
Anoda
Anthriscus cerefolium
Asperula
Atriplex hortensis sr to e-su SU
Baileya
Bassia l-sr
Borago **
Brassica oleracea su
Briza **
Bromus
Caiophora
Calendula ** CL
Callirhoe sr
Callistephus m-sr
Carthamus at 10°C/50°F
Catananche m-sr
Centaurea **
Chrysanthemum sr-e-su ** CL
Cladanthus m-sr
Clarkia e-sr at 15°C/59°F **
Cleome
Coix
Collinsia at 15°C/59°F **
Collomia at 15°C/59°F **
Consolida at 10°C/50°F SU ** CL
Convolvulus m-sr
Coreopsis e-sr to e-su SU
Coriandrum e-l sr
Cosmos bipinnatus l-sr

Crepis CF
Cuphea l-sr
Cynoglossum m-sr
Dianthus at 13°C/55°F
Dimorphotheca m-sr
Downingia
Dracocephalum m-sr
Echium
Emilia l-sr
Eragrostis m-sr
Erysimum l-sr to e-su
Eschscholzia SU T ** CL
Euphorbia
Gaillardia l-sr-e-su
Gaura
Gilia m-sr **
Glaucium T **
Gypsophila T
Helianthus at 15°C/59°F e-sr T
Heliophila sr -e-su SU
Heliotropium at 16°C/61°F
Hordeum **
Hunnemannia m-sr
Iberis SU **
Impatiens glandulifera
Ionopsidium sr-su ** KF
Ipomoea warm climates only
SO 24 hrs
Ipomopsis at 13°C/55°F
Isatis at 13°C/55°F
Koeleria
Lagurus ** CF
Lamarckia SU
Lathyrus odoratus CF SO ** CL
Lavatera m-l sr
Layia **
Legousia m-sr **
Leucanthemum **

Limnanthes ** CL
Limnocharis WS
Linanthus **
Linaria e-sr
Lindheimera m-sr, CF e-sr ** CL
Linum **
Loasa l-sr
Lobularia l-sr
Lonas **
Lupinus CH/SO 24hrs seedbed
Lychnis
Malcolmia l-sr SU
Malope
Malva e-sr-e-su
Matthiola longipetala ssp bicornis SS
Mentzelia **
Micromeria l-sr
Milium
Mimulus CF **
Moluccella l-sr
Myosotis arvensis
Myosotis or CF e-su
Nemophila **
Nicandra m-sr
Nigella m-sr ** CL
Nolana l-sr
Omphalodes
Orychophragmus
Oryza SS at 19-24°C/66-75°F, WT
Panicum
Papaver e-m sr T **
Petroselinum crispum l-sr at
15°C/59°F ^
Phacelia
Phacelia tanacetifolia D
Phlox drummondii at 15°C/59°F
Physalis m-sr
Platystemon
Polypogon **
Pteropogon l-sr
Reseda ** CL
Rhodanthe m-sr
Rumex
Sanvitalia **
Satureja hortensis
Scabiosa m-sr
Sedum m-sr

Setaria **
Silene HA **
Silybum e-sr N
Tagetes l-sr
Thymophylla m-l-sr
Tithonia l-sr T
Tolpis
Trachymene l -sr ^
Triticum **
Tropaeolum
Tuberaria m-l sr
Zinnia l-sr SU

SOWING BIENNIALS DIRECT

Biennials are often sown in outdoor nursery beds and then transplanted into their final flowering positions. Sow from spring to midsummer and transplant in autumn.

Alcea SD m-su N
Anchusa capensis at 13°C l-wi to e-sr
Anethum SD, SU
Angelica seedbed or CF au
Anthriscus
Calceolaria SS at 18°C sr -su
Campanula medium SS at 15°C ** CL
Carthamus at 16°C/61°F
Carum SD au MO T
Chelidonium SD, e-sr
Cirsium CF
Cynoglossum SD, m-sr
Dianthus SD l-sr /e-sr at 13°C/55°F
Digitalis purpurea SD/CF l-sr
Dipsacus SD **
Echium at 13°C su
Erysimum seedbed l-sr to e-su
Euphorbia seedbed l-sr to e-su
Gentianopsis SD, SS
Glaucium
Heliophila sr SU
Hesperis
Ipomopsis aggregata at 13°C/55°F

e-sr or e-su
Isatis at 13°C/55°F
Lavatera CF m-su
Lunaria annua e-su
Malva
Matthiola at 13°C/55°F
Michauxia
Myosotis CF or seedbed l-sr to e-su
Oenothera SD au, e-su CF
Onopordum SD or CF au or sr
Orychophragmus violaceus SD sr
or e-su
Papaver SD l-sr to e-su T
Petroselinum
Psylliostachys at 16°C/61°F
Rudbeckia at 16°C/61°F
Salvia CF, SD su
Scabiosa SD m-sr, or 6-12°C e-sr
Sedum at 16°C, or SD m-sr
Silybum l-sr - e-su N
Smyrnium l-sr
Verbascum CF l-sr or e-su N
Viola CF l-wi to e-sr or su

OUTDOOR NURSERY BEDS

A large number of seedlings can be raised in containers in an outdoor nursery bed. The beds suppress weed and isolate young plants from any soil-borne diseases. Containers can drain freely and water is easily accessible through capillary action. Sand beds require the least watering.

To prepare a nursery bed

Level a site, enclose it with 8cm (3in) high wooden boards, then line it with water-permeable fabric or sand.

Biennials

Biennials are sown in a specially prepared seed bed in a corner of the garden. Transplant seedlings to 15cm (6in) apart to produce bushy plants.

They should be discarded after the second year when they have flowered. Biennials normally produce vast quantities of seed.

SOWING OTHER GENERA DIRECT

This list includes all other genera which can be sown direct including perennials, trees, shrubs, herbs.

Althaea m-su
Ammobium m-sr
Bellevalia au
Bellis su
Berberis e-sr
Briza sp/su
Calla MS
Callirhoe e-sr
Carlina au
Chamaemelum
Coreopsis seedbed m-sr
Deschampsia sr **
Elymus sr **
Foeniculum
Glaucium
Heliophila sr
Hordeum
Humulus japonicus and cvs l-sr
Hunnemannia e-sr, au KF
Hyacinthella
Hyoscyamus
Koeleria
Linanthus au
Lunaria per
Malva e-sr-e-su
Medicago **
Melica
Milium
Muscari au
Monarda l-sr
Nelumbo SC at 25°C/77°F, MS
Nolana l-sr
Pilosella
Platycodon
Rumex
Scopiola **
Scrophularia **
Trachelium HHspp l-sr

SOWING COLD - AUTUMN

The following genera which include perennials, trees, shrubs and alpines can all be sown cold in autumn.

These are normally sown in pots in a cold frame, an open frame or outdoors in pans (particularly in the case of alpines), or in a seedbed (usually for tree seed). Protect from mice. Most seeds will benefit from a layer of vermiculite if they are to stand a long time. A layer of fine grit is preferable for alpines. Some species, especially if seed is sown fresh will germinate quickly, others need a period of cold, or even exposure to frost before they will germinate. It is wise to keep pots of most species at least two years, longer if you can.

Abies ST 21 days
Acaena
Achillea
Acinos
Aconitum * ^
Actaea ^
Actinidia *
Adenocarpus *
Aethionema
Ajuga
Alchemilla EC
Alkanna
Althaea
Alyssum *
Amorpha SC, OF
Ampelopsis ST, OF
Amsonia *
Anacyclus OF
Androsace OF
Andryala *
Angelica
Antennaria * OF
Anthericum *
Anthriscus *
Anthyllis
Aquilegia *
Arabis *
Aralia ST
Arctostaphylos B
Arenaria OF *
Arisaema *
Armeria *
Arnica
Aronia in seedbed

Artemisia *
Arthropodium *
Arum N
Aruncus *
Asimina ST 90 days
Asperula OF
Aster *
Asteranthera SS
Astilbe EC
Astilboides
Aubrieta *
Aucuba
Aurinia
Azorella OF
Balsamorhiza
Bellevalia
Berchemia *
Berkheya
Betula in seedbed
Bidens e-au
Blechnum spores late summer
Boenninghausenia
Boltonia
Broussonetia
Buglossoides *
Buxus
Calandrinia alp
Calceolaria hardy spp *
Callicarpa *
Campanula *
Campsis
Cardamine
Carex other than NZ spp
Carmichaelia * SC

Carpinus in seedbed
Caryopteris
Cassiope OF
Catalpa OF
Ceanothus OF, seedbed
Celtis OF
Cephalanthus hardy spp
Cephalotaxus * ST ^
Cerastium OF *
Cercis
Cestrum frost-hardy spp
Chaenomeles OF/seedbed
Chaenorhinum
Chamaecytisus *
Chiastophyllum
Chionanthus ^
Chionodoxa
Cichorium *
Cimicifuga
Cladrastis OF
Claytonia OF
Clethra hardy spp
Clintonia
Codonopsis *
Colutea *
Coluteocarpus
Convallaria seedbed ^
Cornus in seedbed, * ST
Corydalis T
Corylopsis OF
Cotinus
Crambe *
Cyathodes
Cydonia in seedbed
Cynoglossum *
Cytisus *
Dacrydium
Danae
Darmera *
Decaisnea OF
Dendranthema
Desmodium
Deutzia
Dianthus alp *
Dietes
Digitalis
Dipelta *

Diplarrhena *
Dipteronia in seedbed
Dirca
Disanthus *
Discaria *
Disporopsis *
Disporum
Docynia
Dracocephalum *
Drimys
Duchesnea *
Edgeworthia
Edraianthus OF
Elaeagnus
Eleutherococcus seedbed
Ephedra OF hardy spp
Eremurus
Erinacea OF
Erinus OF
Eriogonum OF
Eriophyllum OF
Eritrichium OF
Eryngium *
Eucomis at 16°C/61°F
Eucommia seedbed
Euphorbia EC *
Exochorda seedbed
Fabiana *
Fagus seedbed * ST
Fendlera * 13°C
Ferraria at 6-12°C/43-54°F
Festuca au-sr
Filipendula
Fothergilla ^
Fraxinus OF, ST 2-3 mths
Freesia SO 24 hrs, dark BH 13°C
Fritillaria EC, CG, FT N
Gagea
Galax OF, ER
Galega
Garrya *
Gaultheria
Gaylussacia
Genista *
Geum *
Gevuina
Gillenia *

Gleditsia OF, SC
Globularia
Gymnocladus SC or SO
Halesia at 14-25°C/57-77°F, then to CF after 60 days
Halimodendron
Helonias OF
Heloniopsis *
Hemerocallis *
Hieracium OF
Hoheria
Horminum OF
Hovenia * SC
Hyacinthella
Hydrocotyle au to sr
Hypericum
Hyssopus
Iberis
Idesia
Ilex
Indigofera
Iris SO 48 hrs *
Isatis * at 13°C/55°F
Ixia KF
Jancaea
Kalopanax
Kelseya OF
Kitaibela *
Koelreuteria
Laburnum
Lamium
Lathyrus SO
Laurus at 18°C/64°F BH
Leontopodium *
Leucanthemum *
Leucojum
Levisticum
Lewisia
Leycesteria
Liatris
Ligularia *
Ligustrum *
Lindera
Linnaea
Linum *
Liquidambar
Liriodendron

Liriope
Lithocarpus
Lithophragma
Lloydia (FT as Fritillaria)
Lotus * Hspp
Lupinus * sm spp/ alp
Luzula *
Lycium
Lyonia
Lyonothamnus
Maackia
Magnolia ST
Mahonia ST
Malus seedbed
Marrubium *
Maytenus UG
Mazus *
Medicago
Meliosma
Menispermum
Menziesia
Merendera for sr flowering spp
Mertensia DC, SH
Mespilus seedbed
Metasequoia seedbed
Microbiota seedbed
Mimulus H spp
Mitchella DC
Mitella
Moltkia
Monarda *
Monardella UG
Moraea HHspp UG
Morus
Mukdenia
Muscari
Mutisia fr-H, HH at 16°C/61°F
Myrrhis odorata or wi ^
Myrsine
Myrteola OF
Myrtus
Nectaroscordum
Nepeta
Nothofagus seedbed
Notholirion
Notospartium *
Nyssa seedbed

Olsynium
Omphalodes lucilliae
Ononis *
Onosma OF
Origanum
Ornithogalum *
Osteomeles
Oxalis at 13°C/55°F
Oxydendrum
Pachyphragma
Pachystegia
Paeonia DE
Paliurus
Paris
Parrotia
Parthenocissus
Paulownia *
Petrocallis OF
Petrophytum OF
Petrorhagia
Petteria
Phacelia sericea
Phellodendron
Photinia
Phuopsis OF
Physocarpus *
Physoplexis OF
Physostegia
Picrasma
Pieris *
Piptanthus *
Plantago
Platanus seedbed
Platycarya
Poa *
Podophyllum
Polemonium
Poliothyrsis
Polygala Hspp
Polygonatum ^
Poncirus
Potentilla *
Prinsepia
Prunus
Pseudocydonia

Pseudopanax Hspp *
Ptelea *
Pterocarya
Pteroceltis
Pterocephalus
Pterostyrax
Pulsatilla
Puschkinia or su
Pyracantha
Pyrus OF, seedbed
Ranunculus SG, PG ^ alp spp
Ranzania
Rheum
Rhodiola *
Rhodothamnus OF
Rhodotypos
Rhus seedbed
Robinia
Rohdea
Romulea at 6-12°C/45-54°F
Sagina
Sambucus
Sanguinaria
Sanguisorba ^
Santolina
Saponaria *
Sarcococca *
Saxifraga OF
Schima at 6-12°C/45-54°F
Scilla
Scutellaria
Sedum Hspp
Sesleria
Shepherdia
Sibiraea *
Sidalcea *
Silene
Sinocalycanthus
Sinofranchetia
Sinojackia
Sinowilsonia
Sisyrinchium *
Skimmia
Smilacina EF ^
Smilax

Sorbaria
Sorbus
Spartium
Stachys *
Stachyurus
Staphylea
Stewartia
Stokesia *
Stylophorum
Succisa *
Symphytum *
Symplocos
Synthyris OF
Tetracentron seedbed
Tetradium seedbed
Tetrapanax
Thuja l-wi
Thujopsis l-wi
Tiarella
Tolmiea
Toona
Tripetaleia
Trochodendron
Tulipa EF
Ulex *
Ulmus *
Umbellularia
Vaccinium
Veronica
Veronicastrum
Vestia
Viburnum or seedbed
Vigna *
Vitis *
Waldsteinia *
Weigela
Wikstroemia
Wulfenia *
Xanthoceras
Xanthorhiza
Xerophyllum *
Zanthoxylum
Zelkova
Zenobia l-wi

SOWING IN A SEEDBED

If you do not have the facilities to sow seed under cover or you have no provision to provide aftercare for seedlings, you may wish to sow in a seedbed.

Preparing the site

A seedbed must be sheltered. Protect from wind if possible with a hedge or an artificial windbreak.

The ground must be prepared thoroughly, it must be free of weed. Make preparations in advance, preparing the soil in the spring and summer and hoeing off weed seedlings as they appear. Incorporate well-rotted leaf mould at this stage, it will greatly improve the soil structure. Dig to one spade depth.

A raised bed

Prepare a raised bed, 10-20cm (4-8in) deep and 1m (3ft 9 in) wide. Earth up the soil or place boards around the area. This will provide a well-drained soil. Mark drills 10-15cm (4-6in) apart with a hoe, cane or by pressing the straight side of a board into the soil.

Sowing seed

Rake over the surface and firm the soil. Most tree seeds are large and can now be easily space-sown into drills or use a dibber. Small seed always needs to be sown in drills, sow thinly to avoid the risk of fungal attack. Sow from early to mid spring or in cooler climates for seed which needs cold treatment, in mid to late autumn. Cover the seeds by roughly twice their own diameter. Large seed needs to be sown at least 5-8cm (2-3in) deep. Draw the soil lightly over the seeds. Rake a 2cm deep layer of medium grit over the entire seedbed. If necessary thin seedlings. Leave the seedlings to grow on for up to a year

SOWING COLD -SPRING

The following genera usually germinate better with a spring sowing in the cold frame.

Acanthus
Aethionema
Ajania
Alchemilla
Alyssum
Anagallis
Anaphalis
Anchusa
Andropogon
Anisotome
Anthemis
Aphyllanthes
Aponogeton
Arisarum
Aristotelia
Armeria
Arundo
Asclepias tender spp in heat l-wi.
Asphodeline
Asphodelus N
Aubrieta
Baccharis
Belamcanda
Bellis m-su
Berberidopsis
Bothriochloa
Bouteloua
Boykinia
Briggsia PS
Bruckenthalia
Brunnera
Buphthalmum
Bupleurum
Calamintha
Calocedrus
Caloscordum
Catananche N
Cedrus PC 21 days
Centaurea
Centranthus
Cephalaria
Chamaecyparis seedbed

Chasmanthium
Chelone
Chionochloa
Cicerbita
Cirsium
Conandron SS
Coprosma
Cryptomeria
Cunninghamia
Cupressus
Cynara
Cyperus DC hardy spp
Digitalis
Doronicum
Draba
Dregea
Echinops seedbed m-sr
Eomecon
Eragrostis
Eranthis l-sr
Erigeron
Erysimum
Eupatorium hardy spp
Fallopia
Fitzroya
Galega SO overnight
Galium
Gaura
Gillenia
Gladiolus HA spp
Glaucidium OF
Glycyrrhiza
Goniolimon m-sr
Grindelia
Gypsophila
Hedyotis
Helenium
Helianthus
Helichrysum
Helictotrichon
Heliopsis
Heterotheca e-sr, FF

Heuchera
Hippocrepis SC or au
Holboellia
Hosta
Hottonia MS
Hydrangea
Incarvillea
Inula
Ipheion su
Juniperus **
Knautia
Kniphofia
Lardizabala
Larix seedbed
Lavandula
Leiophyllum SS
Lespedeza
Leucothoe
Libocedrus
Limonium
Linaria
Lindelofia
Lloydia OF
Luma
Lunaria rediviva
Lysimachia
Macleaya
Malvastrum
Marrubium ^
Matthiola
Meehania
Melicytus
Melissa
Mentha
Merendera for au fl spp
Micromeria
Miscanthus
Mitraria
Molinia
Moraea frost H spp
Morisia
Myosotis
Oenothera per, an
Omphalodes
Orixa
Ourisia PG
Papaver

Peltoboykinia
Penstemon rock gdn spp
Persicaria
Phygelius KF
Physalis
Picea
Pimelea
Pinus
Potentilla
Primula SS HHspp
Prumnopitys
Pseudolarix
Pseudotsuga
Putoria
Raoulia PG
Ratibida
Retama
Rhodanthemum
Rodgersia
Roscoea
Rosmarinus
Rudbeckia
Ruta
Saccharum
Salvia Hspp
Sapindus Hspp ST 8 wks
Sciadopitys
Scopiola
Sempervivum
Sequoia
Sequoiadendron
Seriphidium
Sideritis Hspp
Sorghastrum
Stenotus
Stipa
Taxodium
Thymus
Trifolium
Trollius
Tropaeolum KF ^
Tsuga
Valeriana
Verbascum
Vernonia
Zauschneria

SOW AS SOON AS RIPE

Sow the following as soon as ripe. Some suppliers sell fresh seed, or you can beg or borrow from friends.

Most of the seeds of the genera that follow have a very short viability or can germinate rapidly, even on the stem of the plant and therefore need to be soon as soon as ripe. They will germinate much better in this way, although many of them can also be sown in spring, but they will probably not germinate as well as seed sown fresh as soon as ripe, so expect a poorer germination. Many genera can be sown cold, but some require heat.

Acantholimon
Acanthostachys at 27°C/81°F
Acca at 14°C/57°F
Acer
Aciphylla
Acmena at 14°C/57°F
Adansonia at 21°C/70°F
Adenia at 21°C/70°F
Adenium at 21°C/70°F
Adenophora
Adiantum N**
Adlumia
Adonis PG ^
Aeonium at 21°C/70°F
Aeschyanthus at 21°C/70°F
Aesculus
Agapanthus *
Aglaomorpha N**
Aglaonema at 21°C/70°F
Ailanthus *
Akebia
Albuca at 16°C/61°F
Aleurites *
Alisma N
Allium *
Alluaudia at 21°C/70°F
Alnus in seedbed
Alocasia at 23°C/73°F
Aloe at 21°C/70°F
Alopecurus *
Alpinia at 20°C/68°F
Alstroemeria at 20°C/70°F 4 wks,
CH resow at 10°C/50°F T
Alternanthera at 16°C/61°F *
Amaryllis at 16°C/61°F

Amelanchier
Amorphophallus at 21°C/70°F
Anacampseros at 18°C/64°F
Androsace
Anemone CS TH PG ^
Anemonella su
Anemonopsis macrophylla EC ^
Angelica EX
Anigozanthos ^ SO
Antennaria
Anthurium ^
Aporocactus
Aralia
Araucaria in seedbed
Araujia *
Arbutus
Arisaema CS ^
Arisarum at 15°C/59°F
Aristolochia at 16°C for hardy sp,
24°C for tender sp.
Arnebia
Arum CS
Asarum
Asplenium spores at 15°C for
hardy spp, 21°C for tender spp.
Astelia
Astrantia
Athyrium spores at 15°C for
hardy spp, 21°C for tender spp.
Azorella **
Babiana at 15°C/59°F
Baptisia
Barbarea bi
Begonia spp 20°C/68°F SS * N
Billardiera 13°C/55°F *

Billbergia 27°C/81°F
Bloomeria
Bolax
Bolbitis spores at 21°C
Bongardia
Boykinia
Brachychiton at 16°C/61°F
Brachyscome per at 18°C/64°F
Brimeura
Briza at 10°C/50°F
Brodiaea 13°C/55°F
Bromelia 27°C/81°F
Bulbinella
Bulbocodium SH, EF
Butomus MS
Callianthemum
Calochortus EF, dry
Calomeria 13°C/55°F
Caltha PS, DC
Calycanthus
Camassia
Canistrum at 27°C/81°F
Caragana SO
Cardiocrinum
Carissa at 18°C/64°F *
Carya SD
Castanea
Castanopsis
Catopsis
Caulophyllum OF, ^
Celastrus OF
Celmisia OF at 10°C/70°F
Centaurium **
Ceraria
Cercidiphyllum OF
Chaerophyllum *
Chasmanthe at 13°C/55°F
Cheilanthes spores at 16°C/61°F
Chimaphila ER, SH
Chimonanthus
Chionodoxa
Chrysogonum
Chrysolepis
Cibotium spores at 21°C/70°F
Cimicifuga
Cinnamomum at 16°C/61°F
Cistus *

Claytonia SH
Clematis
Clivia at 21°C/70°F
Codonopsis
Colchicum OF, EF, SH
Coniogramme spores at 16°C/61°F
Convallaria R
Coptis
Coriaria
Coronilla * ST, 13°C
Cortusa OF
Corydalis ^ OF *
Corylus in seedbed
Costus at 21°C/70°F
Cotoneaster
Crataegus R in seedbed or * ST ^
Cremanthodium
Crepis at 10°C/50°F
Crinum at 21°C/70°F *
Crocosmia
Crocus
Cryptanthus at 27°C/81°F
Ctenanthe at 21°C/70°F *
Curcuma at 21°C/70°F
Cyananthus OF *
Cyathea spores at 16°C/61°F
Cyclamen D at 16°C/61°F SO 10 hrs
Cyclamen o-p cvs D l-su at
16°C/61°F SO 10 hrs
Cyclamen other cvs D l-wi to m-sr
at 16°C/61°F SO 10 hrs
Cyclamen persicum D at 16°C/
61°F SO 10 hrs
Cypella at 7-13°C/45-55°F
Cyrilla
Cyrtanthus at 16°C/61°F
Cyrtomium spores at 16°C/61°F
Cystopteris spores at 16°C/61°F
Damasonium MS
Daphne
Davallia spores at 15°C for hardy
spp, 21°C for tender spp.
Davidia WF, OF
Deinanthe ^
Dennstaedtia spores at 15°C for
hardy spp, 21°C for tender spp.
Diascia

Dicentra *
Dichelostemma at 16°C/61°F *
Dicksonia spores at 15°C
Dicranostigma
Dictamnus
Didymochlaena spores at 21°C
Dierama
Dionysia
Diospyros OF
Dipcadi
Diphylleia
Diplazium spores at 21°C
Discocactus at 27°C/81°F
Distylium
Dodecatheon EC
Doodia spores at 15°C
Doryopteris spores at 21°C
Draba
Drosera 13°C/55°F
Dryas
Drynaria spores at 21°C/70°F
Dryopteris spores at 15°C
Echeveria at 18°C/64°F
Ehretia
Elettaria at 21°C/70°F
Elsholtzia at 13°C/55°F
Epigaea at 13°C/55°F SS WB
Epilobium
Epimedium
Episcia at 24°C/75°F
Eranthis
Erinus
Erodium OF
Eryngium
Erythronium
Etlingera at 21°C/70°F
Eucharis at 25°C/77°F
Eucomis at 16°C/61°F KF 2 yrs
Eucryphia
Euonymus
Euphorbia frost tender succ at
16°C/61°F
Euphorbia hardy per *
Euptelea
Eurya
Ferula T
Firmiana at 10°C/50°F

Fockea
Franklinia at 16°C/61°F
Galanthus KS
Galium SH
Galtonia KF 2yrs
Geissorhiza
Gentiana OF
Geranium per, H spp
Ginkgo
Gordonia
Gunnera KF ^
Gymnocarpium spores at 15°C
Gynandriris KF wi
Haastia WB
Habranthus at 16°C/61°F
Hacquetia
Haemanthus at 16°C/61°F
Hakea SI at 16°C/61°F
Hamamelis
Haplopappus
Hebe
Hedychium at 21°C/70°F
Hedysarum *
Helianthemum *
Helichrysum alp OF
Helleborus
Hemionitis spores at 21°C/70°F
Hepatica OF
Herbertia at 15°C/59°F *
Hippeastrum at 16°C/61°F
Hippophae *
Hohenbergia at 24°C/75°F
Hohenbergiopsis at 24°C/75°F
Holodiscus OF
Houttuynia
Howea at 27°C/81°F
Hyacinthoides SH
Hydrocharis WT
Hydrocleys at 20°C/70°F WT
Hylomecon
Hymenocallis at 21°C/70°F
Hypoxis at 10°C/50°F *
Ipheion *
Iris
Isopyrum OF
Itea OF
Ixia

Ixiolirion
Jasione
Jeffersonia
Juglans or * ST
Juniperus R
Kaempferia at 20°C/68°F
Kirengeshoma * ^
Lachenalia at 16°C/61°F
Lagenophora
Lathraea H
Leontice
Leontopodium OF **
Leptinella
Leucanthemopsis OF
Leucocoryne
Leucogenes
Leucojum *
Leucopogon
Levisticum seedbed
Lewisia
Libertia
Lilium 16°C/55°F HHspp
Lilium CF Hspp
Lobelia per
Lomandra 16°C/55°F
Lomatium
Lonicera H spp
Lophomyrtus 16°C/55°F
Loropetalum
Lychnis *
Lycoris at 6-12°C/45-54°F
Lygodium spores at 21°C
Lysichiton DC
Macfadyena at 16°C/61°F *
Maclura OF
Macropidia at 10°C/50°F
Macrozamia at 21°C/70°F
Maianthemum
Mandragora
Manglietia at 5-9°C/41-48°F
Maranta at 16°C/61°F
Margyricarpus
Matteuccia at 15°C/59°F
Mazus at 10°C/50°F
Meconopsis MO *
Megacodon
Melica

Melittis *
Merendera
Meum
Michelia
Microcachrys
Microlepia spores at 20°C/68°F
Millettia at 6-12°C/45-54°F
Mimetes at 6-12°C/45-54°F
Monstera
Moraea
Morina SI, PG
Muehlenbeckia at 21°C/70°F
Musa at 21°C/70°F, SO 24 hrs
Myoporum at 6-12°C/45-54°F
Myosotidium
Myrica
Myrrhis *
Nandina
Narcissus DP, KF, M 2yrs N
Nectaroscordum
Neolitsea
Neopaxia
Neoregelia at 27°C/81°F
Nepenthes MC, WT at 24°C/75°F
Nephrolepis spores at 21°C
Nerine at 10°C/50°F
Nidularium at 27°C/81°F
Nomocharis at 10°C/50°F
Notholirion
Nothoscordum
Nymphaea SS, MS at 10°C
H spp, 27°C tropical spp
Ochagavia at 27°C/81°F
Oemleria seedbed
Omphalogramma OF
Onoclea spores at 15°C
Ophiopogon
Ornithogalum
Orontium WT
Osmanthus
Osmunda at 15°C within 3 days
Ostrowskia SI
Ostrya seedbed or CF
Ourisia PG *
Ozothamnus
Pamianthe at 18°C/64°F
Pancratium at 16°C/61°F

Pandanus at 18°C/64°F * SO
24 hrs
Paradisea
Parahebe *
Paraquilegia PG
Patrinia
Pellaea spores at 15°C
Pentachondra at 16°C/61°F
Pentaglottis *
Peperomia at 21°C/70°F
Perezia
Petrocosmea at 16°C/61°F
Phaedranassa
Phegopteris spores at 15°C
Phlebodium spores at 21°C
Phlox per
Physaria
Pimpinella
Pinellia
Pinguicula SS, SM at 15°C
Pittosporum *
Pityrogramma spores at 21°C
Platycerium at 21°C/70°F
Plectranthus at 21°C/70°F
Podocarpus
Podophyllum
Polianthes at 21°C/70°F
Polypodium spores at 16°C/61°F
Polystichum spores at 16°C/61°F
Pontederia
Potentilla
Primula Hspp
Protea at 16°C/61°F *
Psilotum spores at 21°C
Pteris spores at 21°C
Pulmonaria
Pulsatilla
Puya at 21°C/70°F
Pyrola SS, SM
Pyrrosia spores at 21°C
Quercus
Quesnelia at 27°C/81°F
Ramonda VT ^
Ranunculus
Rehderodendron
Reineckea
Rhamnus

Rhodochiton at 16°C *
Rhododendron at 16°C * ER, SS
Rhodohypoxis at 6-12°C/45-54°F *
Rhodophiala at 16°C/61°F
Richea * ^
Romanzoffia
Roscoea *
Rumohra spores at 21°C/70°F
Rupicapnos SG
Ruscus or seedbed
Sadleria spores at 21°C
Sagittaria WT
Saintpaulia at 21°C *
Salvia
Sandersonia
Sarcocapnos
Sarcocaulon at 24°C/75°F
Sarracenia ST cold SS, SM
Sassafras
Saxifraga
Scabiosa *
Scadoxus at 21°C
Schisandra
Scilla
Scoliopus
Selaginella spores at 16°C/61°F
Selenicereus at 16°C/61°F
Selinum SI
Semiaquilegia
Serruria at 18°C/64°F *
Shortia
Silphium
Sisyrinchium
Soldanella MC
Sophora
Sparaxis
Sparganium at 15°C/59°F
Spathiphyllum at 24°C/75°F SM *
Stenanthium
Stenocarpus at 18°C/64°F *
Sternbergia at 13°C/55°F
Strongylodon at 27°C/81°F
Styphelia at 6-12°C/45-54°F *
Styrax at 15°C 3mnths, then
0-5°C 3mnths. KF
Sycopsis ER
Symphyandra or * at 13°C

Synnotia at 16°C/61°F *
Syringa *
Tabebuia at 16°C/61°F *
Talinum at 16°C/61°F *
Tamarix
Taxus or seedbed ^
Tecophilea or CF** KF
Telekia
Tellima *
Telopea
Ternstroemia
Tetranema at 21°C/70°F *
Tetraneuris OF
Teucrium
Thalia at 18°C/64°F DC
Thalictrum *
Thelypteris at 15°C/59°F
Thlaspi OF
Tiarella *
Tigridia at 15°C/59°F *
Tilia seedbed or * ST 3-5mnths
Todea at 21°C/70°F
Torreya or seedbed
Townsendia PG
Trachelium Hspp
Tricyrtis
Tripterygium
Triteleia at 15°C/59°F *
Tritonia at 15°C/59°F
Trollius *
Tropaeolum per ^
Tsusiophyllum
Tulbaghia *
Uncinia
Urginea at 15°C/59°F
Uvularia
Vallea at 6-12°C/45-54°F
Vancouveria
Veratrum
Viola spp *
Vitaliana
Vriesea
Wahlenbergia *
Weldenia
Welwitschia at 21°C/70°F DP
Woodsia spores at 15°C
Woodwardia spores at 16°C/61°F

Xerophyllum ^
Zaluzianskya at 10°C/50°F *
Zantedeschia at 21°C/70°F
Zephyranthes at 13°C/55°F *
Zigadenus at 13°C/55°F *

SOWING SPORES

Spores need to be sown fresh, not when they are still bright green but before they have turned brown.
Make sure all equipment and working surfaces are thoroughly sterilised. Mix two parts sphagnum moss peat with one part coarse sand. Spores are surface-sown thinly. Seal the pot with film or in a plastic bag. Place in a closed propagator in indirect light
Hardy and cool-temperate ferns can germinate at 15-20°C (59-68°F) and tropical ferns at 21-27°C (70-81°F). The offspring appear from 2-26 weeks later and can be moved in patches into sterile seed compost. Put in a new plastic bag , seal and grow on in indirect light and closed conditions until fronds appear. Alternatively, you can patch off much later if you leave the pot until tiny fronds appear. In this case, you must apply a dilute liquid fertiliser each month. Choose a balanced fertiliser and dilute to a quarter of the normal recommended strength. This method produces fronds which are clearly visible and easier to handle.
If the surface of the compost becomes slimy, it might be best to throw the contents away, although one or two ferns may be saved. If the pot has become infested with moss, use a pair of tweezers to tease it out.
When the young fronds are growing well, transplant into a tray of soilless compost, water in carefully and keep in a propagator. Harden off gradually and pot up singly when 5-8cm tall.

ANNUALS UNDER COVER

Frost-tender annuals are grown under cover, either indoors or in the greenhouse to maintain the temperature required for maximum germination and to maintain growth before hardening off and planting out.

A large range of annuals can be raised on a windowsill in a warm room. Temperature and time of sowing varies from genera to genera.

Ageratum at 21°C/70°F
Aichryson at 21°C/70°F
Aira at 10°C/50°F **
Amaranthus at 20°C/68°F m-sr
Amaranthus tricolor at 25°C/77°F m-sr
Anchusa at 16°F/61°F
Anoda at 15°C/59°F e-sr
Anthriscus at 10°C/50°F
Antirrhinum at 16°C/61°F e-sr ** at 4°C
Arctotis at 16°F/61°F e-sr ** UG
Argemone at 21°C/70°F e-sr SI
Bassia at 16°F/61°F SS e-sr
Brachyscome at 18°C/64°F SS
Bracteantha at 18°C/64°F MO
Brassica at 15°C/59°F e-sr
Briza at 10°C/50°F **
Browallia at 18°C/64°F SS e-l sr or l-su
Calandrinia at 16°F/61°F
Calceolaria 18°C/64°F SS
Callistephus at 16°F/61°F e-sr
Capsicum annuum at 21°C/70°F m-l sr
Carthamus 10°C/50°F
Celosia 21°C/70°F m-sr to e-su
Cephalipterum at 18°C/64°F MO
Chirita lavandulacea at 21°C/70°F, SU from l-wi
Chrysanthemum at 15°F/59°F ** CL
Cladanthus at 15°C/59°F e-sr
Cleome 18°C/64°F ^
Coix l-wi or e-sr at 13°F/55°F SI/MO
Convolvulus MO at 13°C/55°F

Cosmos at 16°F/61°F m-sr
Cotula SS at 16°F/61°F
Craspedia at 16°F/61°F
Crotalaria at 16°F/61°F
Cuminum l-wi or e-sr at 16°F/61°F
Cuphea at 16°F/61°F
Delphinium at 13°C/55°F
Dianthus at 13°C/55°F
Dimorphotheca at 18°C/64°F
Dorotheanthus at 18°C/64°F l-wi to e-sr
Downingia elegans at 15°C/59°F
Eccremocarpus at 16°F/61°F l-wi to e-sr
Emilia at 18°F/64°F
Eustoma at 16°F/61°F l-wi **
Exacum affine at 18°C/64°F
Felicia at 18°F/64°F
Gaillardia at 16°F/61°F
Gilia 10°C/50°F
Gomphrena at 16°F/61°F e-sr
Helianthus at 16°F/61°F l-wi SI
Helichrysum at 16°F/61°F
Heliophila at 16°F/61°F e-sr **
Hibiscus trionum at 18°F/64°F SO 1hr
Iberis amara at 16°C/61°F l-wi
Impatiens at 15-18°C/60-64°F
Ipomoea SI at 18°C/64°F, CH or SO 24 hrs
Lagenaria siceria at 21°F/70°F SO e-sr
Lavatera at 13°F/55°F m-sr
Leonotis at 16°F/61°F
Limonium at 16°F/61°F
Loasa at 16°F/61°F m-sr
Lobelia at 18°F/64°F l-wi to e-sr

Lonas annua at 16°F/61°F
Malope at 13°F/55°F e-sr
Malva at 16°F/61°F e-sr
Matthiola incana at 13°F/55°F e-sr
Mimosa at 21°C/70°F
Mimulus at 10°C/50°F
Moluccella laevis EC 1-5°C/34-41°F 2 wks, sow at 16°C/61°F e or m-sr
Nemesia at 15°C/59°F e-l sr
Nicandra at 15°C/59°F e-sr
Nicotiana at 21°C/70°F SS
Nierembergia at 15°C/59°F
Nolana at 13°C/55°F e-sr
Ocimum at 18°C/64°F
Origanum majorana at 13°C/55°F
Panicum at 13°C/55°F
Perilla at 16°F/61°F
Petroselinum crispum at 18°C/64°F BH ^
Petunia at 13°C/55°F ** CL
Phlox at 16°F/61°F
Plumbago at 16°F/61°F
Portulaca at 16°F/61°F m-sr
Primula at 16°C/61°F SS
Proboscidea at 21°C/70°F e-sr
Psylliostachys suworowii at 21°C/70°F
Rehmannia at 13°F/55°F l-wi
Reseda at 13°F/55°F l-wi
Rhodanthe at 16°F/61°F
Rudbeckia at 16°F/61°F
Salpiglossis at 21°C/70°F m-sr
Salvia at 13°C/55°F m-sr
Scabiosa 6-12°C/45-54°F e-sr
Schizanthus at 16°F/61°F m-sr
Schizopetalon at 21°C/70°F
Sedum at 13°F/55°F
Senecio cineraria at 21°F/70°F
Silene at 16°F/61°F
Solanum pseudocapsicum at 18°C/64°F
Sorghum bicolor at 13°F/55°F e-sr
Tagetes at 21°C/70°F e-sr
Tanacetum 10°C/50°F or l-wi or e-sr
Thymophylla 10°C/50°F m-sr
Tithonia at 16°F/61°F m-l-sr

Torenia at 18°C/64°F m-sr
Trachymene at 15°C/59°F m-sr ^
Trapa at 16°C/61°F MS N
Trichosanthes at 20°C/68°F
Tropaeolum at 15°C/59°F e-sr
Ursinia at 15°C/59°F
Verbena at 18°C/64°F l-wi to e-sr ^
Xeranthemum at 16°F/61°F e-sr
Zinnia at 16°C/61°F SI, T
Zizania at 18°C/64°F e-sr N

EXTENDING THE GROWING SEASON

Most annuals grown under cover in spring, can also be sown in autumn at the same temperature for late winter and early spring flowering.

Annuals such as Gaillardia which need artificial heat to germinate in early to mid spring, can often be sown in situ in late spring when the outdoor soil temperature has risen and risk of frost has passed.

SOWING TIP

Later sowings direct outdoors can often catch up with earlier sowings made under cover if the correct temperature cannot be sustained.

If you do not have the space or cannot provide the conditions to sow indoors, wait until the soil is the correct temperature and sow seed outdoors in drills or beds.

OTHER GENERA UNDER COVER

There are a number of tender perennials which need to be raised under cover.

I have had success with most of these on a bright windowsill and certainly think it is worth a try sowing seed in this way. Some of the genera listed here include species which are normally grown an annuals in the U.K., many as bedding plants. They can be brought under cover to survive the winter and planted out again the following spring after danger of frost has passed.

Abelmoschus 15°C/59°F
Abromeitella 27°C/81°F
Abutilon 16°C/60°F
Acacia 18°C/64°F
Acanthus 15°C/59°F KF
Achillea ** 15°C/59°F FF
Achimenes SM e-sr 15°C/59°F FF
Acoelorraphe 27°C/81°F
Acokanthera 21°C/70°F
Adenia 21°C/70°F
Adenium 16°C/61°F
Adromischus 21°C/70°F
Aeonium 21°C/70°F
Aethionema e-sr ** 10°C/50°F
Agapanthus ** 16°C/61°F
Agastache ** 16°C/61°F
Agathis 13°C/55°F
Agathosma 16°C/61°F
Agave 21°C/70°F
Agonis 16°C/61°F
Aichryson 21°C/70°F
Aiphanes 25-30°C/77-86°F
Ajuga 10°C/50°F
Albizia 16°C/61°F
Alcea sr,su 15°C/59°F
Alchemilla HH 16°C/61°F
Allamanda 19°C/66°F
Allium schoenoprasum 18°C/64°F BH
Alocasia 25°C/77°F
Aloe 21°C/70°F
Aloinopsis 21°C/70°F
Alonsoa N 16°C/61°F
Alyogyne 16°C/61°F

Amherstia 21°C/70°F
Amicia 16°C/61°F
Ammobium 13°C/55°F
Amorphophallus 19-24°C/66-75°F
Anacyclus 16°C/61°F
Anagallis 10°C/50°F
Anaphalis 10°C/50°F
Anchusa 10°C/50°F
Anemone 16°C/61°F
Anemopaegma 16°C/61°F
Angelonia 24°C/75°F
Angophora 21°C/70°F
Anigozanthos ^ N 15°C/59°F
Anisodontea 16°C/61°F
Anomatheca 16°C/61°F
Anthemis 15°C/59°F
Anthericum 10°C/50°F
Anthurium ^ 25°C/77°F
Antigonon 16°C/61°F
Antirrhinum ** 15°C/59°F
Aporocactus 21°C/77°F
Aptenia 21°C/77°F
Aquilegia ** 10°C/50°F l-sr
Arabis ** 10°C/50°F
Archontophoenix 24-27°C/75-81°F
Arctotheca 16°C/61°F
Arctotis 16°C/61°F
Ardisia 13°C/55°F
Areca 24-27°C/75-81°F
Arenaria ** 10°C/50°F
Arenga 24-27°C/75-81°F
Argemone 18°C/64°F
Argyroderma PS, EX 21°C/77°F
Ariocarpus 24°C/75°F

Aristea TH   16°C/61°F
Arnica 10°C/50°F
Arrabidaea   16°C/61°F
Artemisia 16°C/61°F
Arthropodium 10°C/50°F
Asarina 16°C/61°F
Asclepias 15°C/59°F
Asparagus 15°C/59°F
Asphodeline 10°C/50°F
Aster   15°C/59°F
Astrantia 10°C/50°F
Astrophytum 21°C/77°F
Atherosperma 13°C/55°F
Aurinia e-sr ** 10°C/50°F
Azorella 10°C/50°F
Azorina 16°C/61°F
Aztekium 16°C/61°F
Backhousia SS 13°C/55°F
Bactris   24-27°C/75-81°F
Baeckia SS 13°C/55°F
Banksia 18°C/64°F
Barleria 16°C/60°F
Bauera 21°C/70°F
Bauhinia 21°C/70°F
Beaucarnea 21°C/70°F
Beaufortia 13°C/55°F
Beaumontia 16°C/61°F
Begonia   21°C/70°F
Belamcanda 15°C/59°F
Bellis 13°C/55°F
Bergerocactus 24°C/75°F
Bertolonia 21°C/70°F
Beschorneria 21°C/70°F
Bessera 21°C/70°F
Biarum 13°C/55°F
Bidens   15°C/59°F
Bignonia 18°C/64°F
Bixa   21°C/70°F
Blandfordia 15°C/59°F
Blossfeldia   21°C/70°F
Boltonia 15°C/59°F
Bolusanthus 13°C/55°F
Bomarea 13°C/55°F
Bombax 21°C/70°F
Borassus 27°C/81°F
Boronia 16°C/60°F
Bowenia 24°C/75°F

Bowiea 21°C/70°F
Brachyscome 18°C/64°F
Brachysema SC 13°C/55°F
Brachystelma 21°C/70°F
Brahea 24°C/75°F
Browallia 18°C/64°F
Brownea 16°C/60°F
Browningia 21°C/70°F
Brugmansia 16°C/60°F
Brunnera 10°C/50°F
Bulbine 18°C/64°F
Buphthalmum 10°C/50°F
Bupleurum 10°C/50°F
Burchardia 16°C/60°F
Bursera 21°C/70°F
Butea 21°C/70°F
Butia 24°C/75°F
Caesalpinia SO 24 hrs 13°C/55°F
Calamintha 10°C/50°F
Calamus 21°C/70°F
Calandrinia 15°C/59°F
Calathea 21°C/70°F
Calceolaria sr /su 16°C/61°F
Calibanus 21°C/70°F
Calliandra 16°C/60°F
Callisia 17°C/63°F
Callistemon SS 16°C/60°F
Callitris 13°C/55°F
Calothamnus SS 16°C/60°F
Calpurnia 13°C/55°F
Calymmanthium   21°C/70°F
Campanula TH ** CF 15°C/59°F
Cananga 21°C/70°F
Canarina 16°C/60°F
Canna CH or SO 24 hrs 21°C/70°F
Cantua 16°C/60°F
Caralluma 18°C/64°F
Cardamine e-sr 10°C/50°F
Cardiospermum 18°C/64°F
Carex NZ spp ** 13°C/55°F
Carlina 15°C/59°F
Carludovica 21°C/70°F
Carnegiea 21°C/70°F
Carpentaria 27°C/81°F
Carpenteria 16°C/61°F
Carpobrotus 15°C/59°F
Caryota 27°C/81°F

Cassia SO   21°C/70°F
Casuarina   18°C/64°F
Catananche   15°C/59°F
Catharanthus 21°C/70°F
Cautleya   18°C/64°F
Cavendishia 16°C/61°F
Cedronella   18°C/64°F
Cedronella canariensis 21°C/70°F
Ceiba 21°C/70°F
Celosia 18°C/64°F
Centaurea   10°C/50°F
Centradenia 18°C/64°F
Centranthus 10°C/50°F
Cephalocereus PG 21°C/70°F
Cephalophyllum   18°C/64°F
Ceraria 21°C/70°F
Cerastium ** 15°C/59°F
Ceratopetalum 18°C/64°F
Ceratozamia 27°C/81°F
Cereus 21°C/70°F
Ceropegia 24°C/75°F
Cestrum tender spp 18°C/64°F
Chamaedorea 27°C/81°F
Chamaemelum 10°C/50°F
Chamaerops 24°C/75°F
Chamelaucium SS 13°C/55°F
Chasmanthe 13°C/55°F
Cheiridopsis 21°C/70°F
Chelone 15°C/59°F
Chirita 21°C/70°F
Chlidanthus ** 16°C/60°F
Chlorophytum 18°C/64°F
Chorisia sr-e-su 21°C/70°F
Chorizema SO 18°C/64°F
Chrysalidocarpus 27°C/81°F
Chrysanthemum   16°F/61°F
Chrysogonum virginianum
10°F/50°F
Chusquea 16°C/60°F
Cionura 16°C/60°F
Cirsium 10°F/50°F
Cissus, succulent spp 21°C/70°F
Citrus 16°C/60°F
Cleistocactus 21°C/70°F
Clerodendrum 16°C/60°F
Clethra 10°C/50°F
Clianthus 16°C/60°F

Clitoria SO 24 hrs 21°C/70°F
Clivia 21°C/70°F
Clusia 21°C/70°F
Clytostoma   16°C/60°F
Cobaea 18°C/64°F
Coccothrinax 27°C/81°F
Cochlospermum 21°C/70°F
Cocos 27°C/81°F
Coleonema SS 16°C/60°F
Colvillea 18°C/64°F
Commelina 16°C/60°F
Congea 18°C/64°F
Conicosia m-sr 21°C/70°F
Conophytum SS, SH 21°C/70°F
Convolvulus 15°C/59°F
Copernicia   27°C/81°F
Copiapoa   21°C/70°F
Cordyline   16°C/61°F
Coreopsis FF 10°C/50°F
Coriaria tender spp 16°C/60°F
Correa 16°C/60°F
Corryocactus 21°C/70°F
Cortaderia   16°C/61°F
Corynocarpus 16°C/60°F
Corypha 27°C/81°F
Coryphantha 21°C/70°F
Costus 21°C/70°F
Cotyledon   21°C/70°F
Crambe   10°C/50°F
Craspedia   10°C/50°F
Crassula   16°C/60°F
Crossandra   16°C/60°F
Crotalaria   16°C/60°F
Crowea e-sr 16°C/60°F
Ctenanthe   18°C/64°F
Cunonia   16°C/60°F
Cuphea   16°C/60°F
Curcuma   18°C/64°F
Cybistax   16°C/60°F
Cycas 27°C/81°F
Cynoglossum 15°C/59°F
Cyperus DC tender spp 21°C/70°F
Cyphomandra 16°C/61°F
Cyphostemma 21°C/70°F
Cyrtostachys 27°C/81°F
Dahlia 16°C/60°F
Dais   16°C/60°F

Darmera 10°C/50°F
Darwinia 16°C/61°F
Dasylirion 21°C/70°F
Decarya 21°C/70°F
Delonix 21°C/70°F
Delosperma SS SH 21°C/70°F
Delphinium 13°C/55°F
Dendromecon 13°C/55°F
Denmoza 21°C/70°F
Dianella CS 15°C/59°F
Dianthus chinensis 15°C/59°F
Diascia FF ** N 15°C/59°F
Dicentra 10°C/50°F
Dichelostemma 16°C/60°F
Dictamnus 15°C/59°F
Dictyosperma 27°C/81°F
Dietes ** 15°C/59°F
Digitalis SS 10°C/50°F
Dillenia 16°C/60°F
Dillwynia SO21°C/70°F
Dionaea WT ^ 13°C/55°F
Dioon VS   25-30°C/77-86°F
Dioscorea ** 21°C/70°F
Diplarrhena 15°C/59°F
Discocactus 21°C/70°F
Disocactus 21°C/70°F
Distictis 18°C/64°F
Dodonaea 18°C/64°F
Dombeya 21°C/70°F
Doronicum 10°C/50°F
Dorstenia 21°C/70°F
Doryanthes 13°C/55°F
Dracaena 21°C/70°F
Drosanthemum SS, SH   21°C/70°F
Dryandra SI 21°C/70°F
Dudleya 21°C/70°F
Duranta 18°C/64°F
Duvallia 21°C/70°F
Dyckia 27°C/81°F
Ebracteola 21°C/70°F
Ecballium 18°C/64°F
Eccremocarpus 16°C/60°F
Echeveria   18°C/64°F
Echidnopsis 21°C/70°F
Echinacea   15°C/59°F
Echinocactus sr- au 21°C/70°F
Echinocereus 21°C/70°F

Echinops 15°C/59°F
Echinopsis 21°C/70°F
Echium 13°C/55°F
Edithcolea 21°C/70°F
Elais SO 7 days ^ 21°C/70°F
Embothrium 16°C/60°F
Encephalartos VS 25-30°C/77-86°F
Ensete F, SO 24 hrs SI ^ 24°C/75°F
Eomecon   10°C/50°F
Epacris SS ^ 13°C/55°F
Ephedra tender spp 13°C/55°F
Epilobium   10°C/50°F
Epiphyllum 21°C/70°F
Episcia SM 21°C/70°F
Epithelantha 21°C/70°F
Eremophila SO 3 days ^16°C/60°F
Eremurus   15°C/59°F
Erigeron 15°C/59°F
Erinus 10°C/50°F
Eriobotrya   13°C/55°F
Eriogonum tender spp 13°C/55°F
Eriostemon t SO   13°C/55°F
Eryngium **CF 10°C/50°F
Erythrina 21°C/70°F
Escobaria 21°C/70°F
Espostoa 21°C/70°F
Eucalyptus sr-su   16°C/60°F
Eucomis 16°C/60°F
Eupatorium tender spp   15°C/59°F
Euphorbia ^ **CF 15°C/59°F
Euryale FS 21°C/70°F
Euryops 13°C/55°F
Eustrephus 16°C/60°F
Evolvulus   18°C/64°F
Fatsia 18°C/64°F
Faucaria 18°C/64°F
Fenestraria 18°C/64°F
Ferocactus   18°C/64°F
Ferraria su ** 6-12°C/43-54°F
Ficus 18°C/64°F
Filipendula 10°C/50°F
Fittonia 18°C/64°F
Foeniculum 16°C/60°F BH
Fortunella 21°C/70°F
Fouquieria 21°C/70°F
Fragaria 18°C/64°F
Frailea 18°C/64°F

Francoa 21°C/70°F
Fremontodendron 16°C/60°F
Fuchsia 21°C/70°F
Furcraea 21°C/70°F
Gaillardia FF 16°C/61°F
Galax urceolata 10°C/50°F
Galega 10°C/50°F
Gardenia 21°C/70°F
Gasteria 21°C/70°F
Gaura 10°C/50°F
Gazania FF 18°C/64°F
Gelsemium 16°C/61°F
Geranium HA spp 16°C/61°F
Gerbera 16°C/61°F
Gesneria 21°C/70°F
Geum 10°C/50°F
Gibbaeum 21°C/70°F
Gillenia 10°C/50°F
Gladiolus HHA spp 15°C/59°F
Glaucium ** 15°C/59°F
Glechoma 10°C/50°F
Globba 21°C/70°F
Gloriosa BH 21°C/70°F
Glottiphyllum l-su 21°C/70°F
Glycyrrhiza SO cold 24 hrs
15°C/59°F
Gomphocarpus 16°C/60°F
Graptopetalum 18°C/64°F
Graptophyllum 21°C/70°F
Grevillea SO or SC 16°C/60°F
Grewia 16°C/60°F
Greyia 16°C/60°F
Griselinia 16°C/60°F
Guzmania 27°C/81°F
Gymnocalycium 21°C/70°F
Gypsophila 15°C/59°F
Haageocereus 21°C/70°F
Haberlea TH 16°C/60°F
Haemanthus BH KF 16°C/60°F
Halimium 21°C/70°F
Hardenbergia SO 24 hrs 20°C/68°F
Harrisia 21°C/70°F
Hatiora 21°C/70°F
Haworthia 21°C/70°F
Hedychium 21°C/70°F

Hedysarum SO 24 hrs 15°C/59°F
Hedyscepe 21°C/70°F
Helenium 15°C/59°F
Helianthus 15°C/59°F
Helichrysum 13-16°C/55-61°F
Heliconia SO 24 hrs 21°C/70°F
Heliocereus 21°C/70°F
Heliopsis 15°C/59°F
Hemerocallis ** 15°C/59°F
Hereroa 21°C/70°F
Hermannia 16°C/60°F
Hesperaloe 16°C/60°F
Hesperantha 16°C/60°F
Hesperocallis 16°C/60°F
Heterocentron 21°C/70°F
Heuchera 10°C/50°F
Hibbertia 21°C/70°F
Hibiscus 16°C/60°F
Holmskioldia 21°C/70°F
Homalocladium 16°C/60°F
Hoodia 21°C/70°F
Hosta 15°C/59°F
Hovea SC or SO 16°C/60°F
Hoya 21°C/70°F
Huernia 21°C/70°F
Humulus 16°C/60°F
Hylocereus 21°C/70°F
Hymenocallis 19°C/68°F
Hymenosporum 16°C/60°F
Hyophorbe 27°C/81°F
Hyphaene 21°C/70°F
Hypocalymma DC 16°C/60°F
Hypoestes 18°C/64°F
Hypoxis 13°C/55°F
Hypsela 6-12°C/43-54°F
Hyssopus officinalis 18°C/64°F BH
Ibervillea e-sr 20°C/68°F
Impatiens 16°C/61°F
Inula 10°C/50°F
Iochroma 13°C/55°F
Ipomoea SI, CH or SO 24 hrs
18°C/64°F
Isoplexis 21°C/70°F
Isopogon SS, SO 24 hrs, CE
21°C/70°F

Jaborosa 13°C/55°F
Jacaranda 16°C/60°F
Jacquemontia 18°C/64°F
Jatropha sr-su 24°C/75°F
Jovibarba e-sr 10°C/50°F
Juanulloa 18°C/64°F
Jubaea 25°C/77°F
Juncus 10°C/50°F
Justicia 16°C/60°F
Kalanchoe 21°C/70°F
Kalmia 6-12°C/43-54°F
Kalmiopsis 6-12°C/43-54°F
Kennedia SO 12 hrs 21°C/70°F
Kigelia 21°C/70°F
Kirengeshoma 10°C/50°F
Kleinia 21°C/70°F
Knautia 15°C/59°F
Knightia 16°C/60°F
Kniphofia 15°C/59°F
Kunzea 16°C/61°F
Lablab 21°C/70°F
Laccospadix 27°C/81°F
Lagerstroemeria 13°C/55°F
Lambertia SI 18°C/64°F
Lamium 10°C/50°F
Lampranthus 21°C/70°F
Lantana 16°C/61°F
Lapageria SO 48 hrs 16°C/61°F
Latania 27°C/81°F
Lawsonia 18°C/64°F
Ledebouria 16°C/61°F
Ledum SS 16°C/61°F
Leea 18°C/64°F
Leipoldtia 21°C/70°F
Lenophyllum 21°C/70°F
Leonotis 21°C/70°F
Lepidozamia 24°C/75°F
Leptospermum 16°C/61°F
Leschenaultia 16°C/61°F
Leucadendron ST 16°C/61°F
Leucanthemum 15°C/59°F
Leuchtenbergia 21°C/70°F
Leucocoryne 21°C/70°F
Leucospermum ST 16°C/60°F
Levisticum ** 16°C/60°F BH
Liatris 15°C/59°F
Libertia 10°C/50°F

Licuala 24°C/75°F
Ligularia 15°C/59°F
Limonium 15°C/59°F
Linaria 15°C/59°F
Linospadix 24°C/75°F
Linum 15°C/59°F
Liriope 10°C/50°F
Lithops 21°C/70°F
Littonia 21°C/70°F
Livistona 24°C/75°F
Lobelia HHP 15°C/59°F
Lodoicea VS, DC 24°C/75°F
Lomatophyllum 21°C/77°F
Lonicera hildebrandiana 16°C/61°F
Lophophora 21°C/70°F
Lophospermum 21°C/70°F
Lophostemon 16°C/61°F
Lotus SO 24 hrs 15°C/59°F
Luculia 16°C/61°F
Lupinus e-sr to m-su SI SO cold
24 hrs 15°C/59°F
Luzula 10°C/50°F
Lychnis e-sr 10°C/50°F
Lysimachia 10°C/50°F
Lythrum 15°C/59°F
Lytocaryum 21°C/70°F
Mackaya 16°C/60°F
Macleania SS 13°C/55°F
Macleaya 15°C/59°F
Maihuenia 21°C/70°F
Malephora 21°C/70°F
Malpighia 21°C/70°F
Malva 10°C/50°F
Malvaviscus 16°C/61°F
Mammillaria 21°C/70°F
Mandevilla 21°C/70°F
Manettia 16°C/61°F
Maranta 18°C/64°F
Marrubium ^ 10°C/50°F
Matucana 21°C/70°F
Maurandella 16°C/61°F
Maurandya 16°C/61°F
Mazus 10°C/50°F
Meconopsis MO 15°C/59°F
Medinilla 21°C/70°F
Megaskepasma 21°C/70°F
Melaleuca 21°C/70°F

Melasphaerula 6-12°C/43-54°F **
Melastoma 6-12°C/43-54°F
Melia 16°C/61°F
Melianthus 16°C/61°F
Melissa 10°C/50°F
Melocactus 21°C/70°F
Menziesia 13°C/55°F
Merremia 21°C/70°F
Metrosideros SS   13°C/55°F
Mikania 13°C/55°F
Milla 16°C/61°F
Mimosa 21°C/70°F
Mimulus ** CF 6-12°C/43-54°F
Mirabilis 16°C/60°F e-sr
Monadenium 21°C/70°F
Monanthes 21°C/70°F
Monarda 10°C/50°F or
18°C/64°F BH
Mucuna 21°C/70°F
Musa F, SO 24 hrs, SI 24°C/75°F
Mussaenda 21°C/70°F
Myosotidium 15°C/59°F
Myosotis e-su 10°C/50°F
Myrtillocactus 21°C/70°F
Nautilocalyx SM 17°C/63°F
Nemesia e-l sr 15°C/59°F
Neobuxbaumia 21°C/70°F
Neolloydia   21°C/70°F
Neomarica   16°C/60°F
Neoporteria 21°C/70°F
Nepenthes   27°C/81°F
Nepeta 10°C/50°F
Nerium 16°C/60°F
Nertera 16°C/60°F
Nicotiana SS 18°C/64°F
Nierembergia 15°C/59°F
Nolina 21°C/70°F
Nomocharis 7-10°C/45-50°F
Nopalxochia 21°C/70°F
Nymania   16°C/60°F
Ochna 16°C/60°F
Odontonema 16°C/60°F
Oenothera 10°C/50°F
Olea   13°C/55°F
Omphalodes ** CF 10°C/50°F
Oophytum   21°C/70°F

Ophiopogon 10°C/50°F
Ophthalmophyllum 21°C/70°F
Opuntia SO ^ 21°C/70°F
Orbea 21°C/70°F
Orbeopsis   21°C/70°F
Oreocereus 21°C/70°F
Origanum SS ^ ** 10°C/50°F
Orostachys 13°C/55°F
Oroya 21°C/70°F
Ortegocactus 21°C/70°F
Orthophytum 27°C/81°F
Orthrosanthus 13°C/55°F
Osbeckia 18°C/64°F
Osteospermum 18°C/64°F
Othonna 18°C/64°F
Oxalis 15°C/59°F
Pachycereus 21°C/70°F
Pachycormus 21°C/70°F
Pachycymbium 21°C/70°F
Pachyphytum 21°C/70°F
Pachypodium 21°C/70°F
Pamianthe   18°C/64°F
Pandorea   16°C/60°F
Panicum   16°C/60°F
Papaver T   10°C/50°F
Parkinsonia 18°C/64°F
Parodia   21°C/70°F
Passiflora   16°C/61°F
Patersonia   16°C/61°F
Pavetta   18°C/64°F
Pavonia   21°C/70°F
Pedilanthus 21°C/70°F
Pediocactus 21°C/70°F
Pelargonium 16°C/61°F l-wi e-sr
Pelargonium F1 hybrids
  21°C/70°F l-wi
Peltophorum 18°C/64°F
Peniocereus 21°C/70°F
Pennisetum e-sr   16°C/61°F
Penstemon border per 16°C/61°F
Pentas 16°C/61°F
Peperomia   21°C/70°F
Pereskia   21°C/70°F
Pericallis   16°C/60°F
Periploca   15°C/59°F
Petrophile   18°C/64°F
Petunia FF ** 16°C/61°F

Phebalium   16°C/60°F
Philodendron SS   21°C/70°F
Phlomis 16°C/60°F
Phlox 15°C/59°F
Phoenix 21°C/70°F
Phormium   18°C/64°F
Phylica 16°C/60°F
Phyllocladus 6-12°C/43-54°F
Phyllodoce e-sr 6-12°C/43-54°F
Physalis CS 15°C/59°F
Phytolacca   16°C/60°F
Pilea   21°C/70°F
Pilosocereus 21°C/70°F
Pinanga   24°C/75°F
Piper 21°C/70°F
Pisonia   16°C/60°F
Pistacia e-sr 25°C/77°F
Pitcairnia   21°C/70°F
Plectranthus 21°C/70°F
Pleiospilos   21°C/70°F
Plumbago   16°C/60°F
Plumeria   18°C/64°F
Podalyria   16°C/60°F
Podranea   16°C/60°F
Polemonium 10°C/50°F
Polygala tender spp 16°C/60°F
Polyscias   21°C/70°F
Pongamia   21°C/70°F
Porana SO   18°C/64°F
Portea 21°C/70°F
Primula **   15°C/59°F
Pritchardia 24°C/75°F
Prostanthera 16°C/61°F
Prunella   10°C/50°F **
Pseudopanax tender spp 21°C/70°F
Pseudowintera 16°C/60°F
Pterocactus 21°C/70°F
Pterodiscus 21°C/70°F
Ptilotus   15°C/59°F
Ptychosperma 24°C/75°F
Pueraria   16°C/61°F
Pulmonaria 10°C/50°F
Pultenaea   16°C/60°F
Punica 16°C/61°F
Pycnostachys 16°C/60°F
Pyrostegia   16°C/60°F
Quaqua   21°C/70°F

Quisqualis 18°C/64°F
Ranunculus asiaticus 15°C/59°F
Raphia 27°C/81°F
Ravenala 21°C/70°F
Rebutia 21°C/70°F
Reinwardtia 16°C/60°F
Rhaphidophora 21°C/70°F
Rhapidophyllum 18°C/64°F
Rhapis 27°C/81°F
Rhexia 16°C/61°F GC
Rhipsalis CS 21°C/70°F
Rhodiola 15°C/59°F
Rhodohypoxis 6°C/45°F
Rhoicissus 13°C/55°F
Rhombophyllum   21°C/70°F
Ricinus SI, SO 24 hrs 21°C/70°F
Rigidella 16°C/61°F GC
Rodgersia SM, SS 10°C/50°F
Romneya 15°C/59°F
Romulea 6-12°C/45-54°F
Rothmannia 16°C/60°F
Roystonea   27°C/81°F
Rudbeckia   10°C/50°F
Ruellia 21°C/70°F
Ruschia 21°C/70°F
Sabal 21°C/70°F
Saintpaulia SM 21°C/70°F
Salvia 16-18°C/61-64°F or BH
Sapindus tender spp 16°C/60°F
Saponaria   10°C/50°F
Saritaea   16°C/61°F
Sarmienta   18°C/64°F
Sarracenia ST 2wks, WT lime-free
  18°C/64°F
Scabiosa 15°C/59°F
Scadoxus BH 16°C/61°F
Scaevola   21°C/70°F
Schefflera   21°C/70°F
Schinus   21°C/70°F
Schizachrium 13°C/55°F
Schizostylis 16°C/61°F
Schlumbergera 21°C/70°F
Schotia 16°C/61°F
Schwantesia 21°C/70°F
Scirpoides MC 6-12°C/43-54°F
Sclerocactus 21°C/70°F
Scrophularia 10°C/50°F

Scutellaria   10°C/50°F
Sedum Hspp 13°C/55°F
Sedum tender spp 16°C/61°F
Selago 13°C/55°F
Selenicereus 18°C/64°F
Semele 16°C/60°F
Senecio 16°C/61°F
Senecio cineraria   21°C/70°F
Senna 21°C/70°F
Sesbania 18°C/64°F
Shortia e-sr LU 10°C/50°F
Sidalcea 10°C/50°F
Sideritis tender spp 16°C/61°F
Silene 10°C/50°F
Sinningia SS 18°C/64°F
Sisyrinchium 15°C/59°F
Smithiantha SM 21°C/70°F
Solandra   16°C/61°F
Solanum   18°C/64°F
Solenopsis   16°C/61°F
Solenostemon SS   24°C/75°F
Solidago 15°C/59°F
Sollya 13°C/55°F
Sparaxis 15°C/59°F
Sparrmannia 15°C/59°F
Spathodea   21°C/70°F
Sphaeralcea 15°C/59°F
Sprekelia 15°C/59°F
Stachys 15°C/59°F
Stangeria SS, VS, DC 27°C/81°F
Stapelia 21°C/70°F
Stapelianthus 21°C/70°F
Stapeliopsis 21°C/70°F
Stauntonia 13°C/55°F
Stenocactus 21°C/70°F
Stenocereus 21°C/70°F
Stenomesson 16°C/61°F
Stephanocereus 24°C/75°F
Stephanotis 18°C/64°F
Stokesia laevis **   15°C/59°F
Stomatium   21°C/70°F
Strelitzia 21°C/70°F
Streptocarpus or l-wi, SM
21°C/70°F
Strobilanthes 16°C/61°F
Stromanthe e-sr   21°C/70°F
Strombocactus 21°C/70°F

Stylidium 16°C/60°F
Stylophorum 16°C/60°F
Sutera 16°C/60°F
Sutherlandia 15°C/59°F
Swainsona SO 15°C/59°F
Syagrus 27°C/81°F
Symphyandra wi/e-sr 15°C/59°F
Symphytum 10°C/50°F
Synadenium 18°C/64°F
Syzygium 16°C/61°F
Syzygium aromaticum 27°C/81°F
Tabernaemontana 18°C/64°F
Tacca SS 25°C/77°F
Tanacetum 10°C/50°F
Tapeinochilus e-sr 20°C/68°F
Tecoma 18°C/64°F
Tecomanthe 18°C/64°F
Templetonia 16°C/60°F
Terminalia   21°C/70°F
Tetranema   18-21°C/64-70°F
Tetratheca   16°C/60°F
Thelocactus 21°C/70°F
Thermopsis SO cold 24 hrs ^ T
10°C/50°F
Thespesia 16°C/60°F
Thevetia 18°C/64°F
Thrinax 27°C/81°F
Thryptomene SS   13°C/55°F
Thunbergia 21°C/70°F
Thymus vulgaris   20°C/68°F BH
Tibouchina 16°C/60°F
Tigridia 13°C/55°F
Tillandsia N 27°C/81°F
Tipuana 15°C/59°F
Titanopsis or e-su 21°C/70°F
Trachycarpus   24°C/75°F
Trachelium H spp 10°C/50°F
Trachelium HHspp 13°C/55°F
Tradescantia Hspp 15°C/59°F
Tradescantia tender spp
18°C/64°F
Trematosperma 21°C/70°F
Trichodiadema 21°C/70°F
Trifolium SO cold 24 hrs
10°C/50°F
Tuberaria e-sr 15°C/59°F
Tweedia 15°C/59°F

Tylecodon 21°C/70°F
Uebelmannia N 24°C/75°F
Uncinia 15°C/59°F
Ursinia 15°C/59°F
Valeriana 10°C/50°F
Veitchia 24°C/75°F
Vellozia 21°C/70°F
Veltheimia **21°C/70°F
Verbascum 15°C/59°F
Verbena FF ** 21°C/70°F
Veronica 15°C/59°F
Victoria N 29-32°C/84-90°F
Viola e-m-sr N 15°C/59°F
Virgilia SO or SC 15°C/59°F
Vitex ** 6-12°C/43-54°F
Wachendorfia ** 16°C/60°F

Wahlenbergia e-sr 15°C/59°F
Washingtonia 24°C/75°F
Watsonia ** 13°C/55°F
Weberocereus 21°C/70°F
Wedelia SA 18°C/64°F
Westringia 16°C/60°F
Wigandia 16°C/60°F
Wittrockia 21°C/70°F
Worsleya 21°C/70°F
Wulfenia e-sr 15°C/59°F
Yucca Hspp 16°C/60°F
Yucca tender spp 21°C/70°F
Zantedeschia SI 21°C/70°F
Zauschneria BH 15°C/59°F
Zephyranthes 15°C/59°F

SOWING UNDER COVER

Many species can be raised on the windowsill. A variety of propagators are available for sowing under cover.

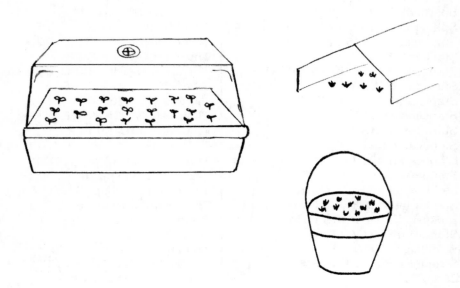

OTHER GENERA TO SOW IN AUTUMN/LATE WINTER

The following can be sown from late winter to early spring.

Abelmoschus   10°C/50°F
Austrocedrus in seedbed
Conophytum SH   21°C/70°F
Enkianthus 21°C/70°F
Eremurus l-wi   15°C/59°F
Farfugium
Fascicularia 27°C/81°F
Freesia   16°C/61°F au/wi
Gypsophila   16°C/61°F wi
Homeria au   16°C/61°F

Hunnemannia   16°C/61°F au
for wi-fl
Melinis   16°C/61°F
Menyanthes wi WT
Morisia monanthos CF
Rehmannia   16°C/61°F
Satureja   16°C/61°F
Tanacetum   10°C/50°F
VIola x wittrockiana

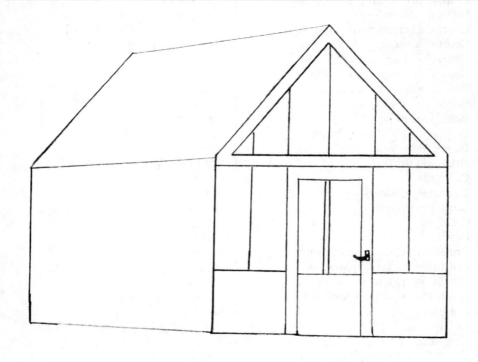

VEGETABLES DIRECT

Sowing vegetables has to be the most rewarding of seed growing. You can actually eat your own produce fresh from the garden. Pick succulent garden produce as and when you want it.

Extend the growing season with horticultural fleece and cloche and you can beat the low-price gluts in the supermarkets and enjoy your vegetables and salads when they are still at top prices in the shops. One of the most wonderful things is that you are not confined to a choice of two or three lettuces, when growing from seed, if you know where to look, you have a choice of over 350 varieties. The choice is not confined to lettuce either, there is a wide range of seed available for all vegetables.

Asparagus pea
Asparagus SO 48 hrs at 85°F, e-sr at 10°C/50°F
Atriplex e-sr SU T
Beans, broad au, e-sr or l-wi
Beans, butter l-sr
Beans, French m-sr to m-su
Beans, haricot m-sr to m-su
Beans, kidney m-sr to m-su
Beans, runner m-sr to e-su
Beans, soya, m-l-sr at 12°C/54°F CL
Beet
Beet, leaf m-sr
Beetroot at 7°C/45°F min
Broccoli or MO
Brussels sprout
Cabbage
Cabbage, Chinese e-su
Cape gooseberry
Cardoon
Carrot
Cauliflower sr- e-su for mini
Cauliflower, su/au sow l-sr
Cauliflower, winter sow e-su
Cauliflower, winter sow l-sr KF
Celeriac
Celery
Chard m-sr **
Chervil, bulbous Nov, germ sr
Chicory, red e-m-su
Chicory, sugar loaf su
Chicory, Witloof sr-e-su
Chrysanthemum greens e-sr to e-su

** at 10°C/50°F
Corn, sweet at 10°C/50°F
Courgette l-sr
Cress, land at 10°C/50°F m to l-su
Cucumber l-sr
Dandelion at 10°C/50°F sr
Endive at 10°C/50°F e-su
Fennel sr or l-su
Garlic
Gherkin at 20°C/68°F
Good King Henry
Ground cherry at 15°C/59°F l-sr
Ice plant l-sr
Jerusalem artichoke
Kale
Kohl rabi sr CL l-su
Lamb's lettuce at 10°C/50°F m to l-su
Leek e-m-sr
Lettuce e-sr to au SU, H cvs l-su to e-au
Marrow l-sr
Melon at 18°C/64°F
Mitsuba
Mizuna l-sr, MO
Mustard
Mustard greens m to l-su, MO
New Zealand Spinach m to l-sr SO
Onion, bulb l-wi to e-sr
Onion, spring e-sr to su, l-su for overwintering
Onion, Welsh at 10°C/50°F sr or l-sr
Pak choi

Parsley, Hamburg e-sr or l-wi at min 12°C/54°F
Parsnip e-sr or l-wi at min 12°C/45°F
Pea at 10°C/50°F SO
Peanut at 16°C/61°F
Potato, sprouted, first early e-sr
Potato, sprouted, main crop l-sr
Potato, sprouted, second early m-sr
Pumpkin l-sr, SO overnight
Purslane, summer at 10°C/50°F KF
Purslane, winter at 10°C/50°F sr, l-su to au
Radish, large m to l-su
Radish, small sr to l-su, SU
Rampion in sand drills at 10°C/50°F e-su
Rhubarb
Rocket, salad at 8-10°C/46-50°F
SU l-wi to e-su, l-su to m-au CL
Salsify at 7°C/45°F e to l-sr
Scorzonera at 7°C/45°F sr or l-su
Seakale at 7°C/45°F ^ sr
Shallot e-sr to l-su
Shungiku
Skirret at 7°C/45°F e to l-sr
Sorrel at 10°C/50°F sr to au
Spinach l-wi to m-su
Squash l-sr
Swede at 10°C/50°F l-sr to e-su
Texel greens at 10-15°C/50-59°F
SU e-sr to e-au, CL
Tomato at 15°C/59°F sr
Turnip e-sr to e-su
Watercress

UNDER COVER

The following vegetables can be sown under cover, either indoors or in a propagator or in the greenhouse, and includes varieties which can be sown later in the year direct outside.

Amaranthus MO at 22°C/71°F or SD
Asparagus pea MO at 10°C/50°F m to l-sr
Aubergine at 25°C/77°F
Bean, Dolichos at 20°C/68°F or SD
Beans, butter at 18°C/64°F e-sr

Beans, French at 12°C/54°F e-sr
Beans, haricot at 12°C/54°F e-sr
Beans, kidney at 12°C/54°F e-sr
Beans, runner at 12°C/54°F e-sr
Beetroot e-sr CL
Brussel sprouts
Cabbage MO
Cape gooseberry at 15°C/59°F
Cardoon SI sr at 10°C/50°F
Carrot at 7°C and above CL
Cauliflower e-su type, sow m-wi at 21°C/70°F, ** CF
Celeriac 15°C/59°F MI
Celery 15°C/59°F MI
Chick pea at 10°C/50°F or SD
Corn salad MO at 10°C/50°F l-sr
Courgette at 20°C/68°F
Cress KP at 15°C/59°F
Cucumber at 20°C/68°F MO, T
Fennel 15°C/59°F BR
Gherkin at 20°C/68°F MO, T
Ice Plant e-sr
Jicama in seedtray at 15°C/59°F
Leek SI m-l wi
Lettuce wi type l-su to l-au, or m-l-wi MO plant out e-sr
Marrow at 20°C/68°F
Melon, sweet 18°C/68°F
Melon, water 22-25°C/72-77°F
Mustard (Brassica hirta) KP at 15°C/59°F
Mustard greens at 15°C/59°F e-au
Okra MI at 20°C/70°F
Peanut MO at 20°C/70°F
Pepper at 21°C/70°F e-sr
Peppers
Potato, sweet at 24°C/75°F
Pumpkin at 20°C/68°F
Radish e-sr
Rhubarb
Salad rape KP at 15°C/59°F
Soya bean
Spinach, Indian at 25°C/77°F or SD
Squash at 20°C/68°F
Tomatillo at 15°C/59°F
Tomato at 15°C/59°F
Turnip l-wi to e-sr

EASY FROM SEED

Many species are not at all difficult to sow. For the majority of these you need no special equipment as many can be sown direct outdoors. There are many that children can enjoy growing such as Helianthus, and easy salad plants such as radish.

Use the individual tables to find out the requirements for each genera listed. Genera usually include many species or varieties and cultivars from which to choose.

Abutilon
Achillea
Adansonia
Adonis
Agastache
Agave
Ageratum
Agrostemma
Albizzia
Alcea rosea
Allocasuarina
Alonsoa
Alyogyne
Alyssoides
Alyssum
Amaranthus
Anethum
Annona
Anthemis
Anthriscus
Aquilegia hybrids such
as 'Long-Spurred'
Arabis blepharophylla
Arctium lappa
Argemone
Aristolochia
Armeria
Asarina
Asperula
Aster
Atractylodes macrocephala
Atriplex hortensis
Aubrieta
Bassia
Belamcanda
Bellis

Bracteantha
Brassica ornamental cabbage
Briza
Bupleurum
Caesalpinia
Calamintha
Calendula
Camassia
Campanula carpatica
Campanula mirabilis
Campanula persicifolia
Campanula takesimana
Campanula thyrsoides
Carthamus
Casuarina
Catananche
Cathartia villosa
Celosia cristata
Centaurea cyanus
Centranthus
Cephalaria
Cerastium
Cereus
Chelone
Chenopodium
Chrysanthemum
Cichorium intybus
Clarkia
Cleome
Commelina
Consolida
Convolvulus
Coreopsis
Coriandrum
Crucianella stylosa
Cuminum

Cymbalaria
Cyperus most
Dahlia merckii
Datura annuals
Daucus carota
Dicranostigma
Digitalis
Dorotheanthus
Echinacea
Echinops
Echinopsis
Echium
Epilobium
Erigeron
Erinus
Eruca vesicaria sativa
Erysimum cheiri
Eschscholzia
Eucalyptus most
Eupatorium
Felicia
Gaillardia
Galega
Galium verum
Gaura
Genista
Geum 'Lady Stratheden'
Geum 'Mrs. Bradshaw'
Gilia
Ginkgo
Gleditsia
Gomphrena
Helenium
Helianthus annuus
Hesperis matronalis
Hibiscus moscheutos
Hosta N
Hyssopus
Iberis amara
Incarvillea
Indigofera
Inula
Ipomopsis
Kalmia
Kniphofia
Koelreuteria
Lablab purpureus

Lactuca
Legousia
Leonurus
Lepidium sativum
Leuchtenbergia
Ligularia
Limnanthes
Limonium latifolium
Linaria most
Linum most
Liquidambar
Loasa
Lobelia
Lonas
Lunaria annua
Lythrum
Malcomia
Malope
Malva sylvestris
Matricaria
Matthiola
Melissa officinalis
Mentha
Mirabilis
Monarda
Myosotis
Nemesia
Nemophila
Nicandra
Nicotiana
Nierembergia
Nigella
Nolana
Nomocharis
Osteospermum
Papaver
Parodias from the formerly
Notocactus group
Passiflora caerulea
Paulownia
Penstemon
Penstemon ovatus
Persicaria
Petrorhagia saxifraga
Phacelia
Phlox
Physalis

Pimpinella anisum
Pinus most
Plantago
Platycodon
Poa
Polemonium
Prunella vulgaris
Psidium
Raphanus
Ratibida
Rebutia
Reseda odorata
Rhodanthe
Ricinus
Rudbeckia most
Rumex
Salvia haematodes
Salvia most
Sanguisorba
Satureja
Schizanthus
Schizopetalon
Scutellaria
Silene
Solanum most
Solenostemon
Sphaeralcea
Spiraea
Stachys byzantina
Steirodiscus
Sutherlandia
Symphyandra
Tagetes
Tanacetum parthenium
Teucrium
Thymus serpyllum
Thymus vulgaris
Tithonia
Torenia
Trigonella
Tropaeolum majus
Tropaeolum peregrinum
Tulbaghia
Verbascum most
Verbascum phoeniceum
Viola tricolor
Xanthium

Xeranthemum
Yucca some
Zaluzianskya

HOW LONG?

Most seed germinates fairly quickly, however it is true that some species take a long time to either germinate or to flower from seed. You will need a great deal of patience to raise these species .

A cold frame is useful, although some species can just be sunk outside in pots. A layer of grit helps protect plants from liverworts and other such things which will be only too happy to inhabit your pots. Mesh will protect the seeds from mice. Sometimes pots will need to be kept for many years.

Remember the process of stratification can be speeded up in your refrigerator which will help with many species.

HOW LONG TO GERMINATE?

Bergenia germinates within 3-6 weeks.
Cephalotaxus takes up to 2 years.
Chionanthus takes up to 18 months.
Convallaria germinates after 2 winters.
Crataegus takes up to 18 months.
Cyathodes takes up to 3 years.
Davidia normally germinates after
2 winters outside.
Epacris takes from 3-6 months.
Eremophila can take from 2 weeks
to more than 2 years.
Fothergilla seed normally germinates
in the second spring after sowing.
Hyphaena is difficult to germinate.
Ilex may take 2-3 years to germinate.
Jubaea may take 3-6 months.
Juniperus may take 5 years .
Mutisia can be difficult.
Osmunda regalis and other spores
germinate reasonably well if sown fresh.
Paeonia may take 2-3 years.
Podocarpus may take 12-18 months.
Ranunculus seed which does not
germinate in the first year may still
do so if the pot is kept for several years.
Stratified Magnolia seed freely.
Stratified Mahonia seed freely.
Taxus may take 2 years or more.
Torreya may take 2 years.
Trillium seedlings usually
appear in the second spring.
Trollius may take 2 years.

HOW LONG TO FLOWER?

Acanthus take 3 years to flower.
Aethionema flower within 2 years.
Agapanthus usually flower in their
3rd year.
Agave take 2-3 years to produce a
small plant.
Asparagus is not difficult from seed,
but you need to wait 3-4 years before
cutting your first spears.
Aster perennials should flower in
their 2nd year.
Bergenia flower after 2 years.
Canna usually flower in their 2nd
year.
Cardiocrinum takes 7 years to flower.
Cephalocereus will not flower until it
is 20 years old.
Clivia take at least 5 years.
Convallaria flower after 3 years.
Cortaderia selloana takes up to 7
years for plumes to form.
Crocus seedlings are best left 2
years before planting out.
Cyclamen cultivars other than
open-pollinated sown in late winter
to early spring will flower in autumn
of the same year.
Cyclamen open-pollinated cultivars
sown in late summer will flower
within 14 months.
Davidia involucrata may take 10
years to flower.

Deinanthe takes several years to reach flowering size.

Delphinium cardinale is quick to flower from seed.

Delphinium may flower from 18 months onwards.

Dianthus barbatus will flower same year from an early summer sowing at 13°C/55°F.

Dionaea may take more than 5 years to flower.

Echinops flower in 2 years.

Epiphyllum take 4-7 years to flower.

Eremurus take 3-5 years to flower.

Eucomis take 3 to 4 years to flower.

Fritillaria seedlings are best left 2 years before planting out.

Galanthus (Snowdrops) take 3 years or more to flower.

Gentiana develop slowly and take between 2 and 5 years to flower.

Gymnocalycium can flower in 2-4 years.

Helianthus perennials take 2-3 years to flower.

Hepatica take 3 years to flower.

Hosta will flower in 2-3 years.

Incarvillea take 3 years to flower, except I. arguta which normally flowers in the first year.

Iris take several years to reach flowering maturity.

Magnolia take many years to flower, M. stellata is the quickest from seed.

Most Codonopsis spp flower in their 3rd year.

Narcissus may take up to 7 years to flower.

Nomocharis takes 4 years to flower.

Olysynium takes 2-3 years to flower.

Ostrowskia magnifica only produces seed leaves in its first year, take care to avoid root damage when potting on, may produce flowers in the 3rd or 4th years.

Pinus edulis takes 25 years to bear cones.

Primula auricula sown in January may flower by the autumn.

Prunus persica (Peach) can take 5-6 years before you see the first fruit.

Punica fruits in 3-4 years.

Ramonda develop slowly, do not pot on until several leaves have formed.

Ranzania take about 4 years to flower.

Rehmannia will flower in 12 to 24 months.

Seedling grasses generally flower within 14 weeks.

Solenostemon makes a pot plant in 3 months.

Stenocarpus take about 7 years .

Strelitzia take 3 years or longer.

Thalictrum take 2-3 years to reach flowering size.

Trillium take 5-7 years to reach flowering size.

Triteleia take 3-5 years to reach maturity.

Tulbaghia reach flowering size within 2 years.

Tulipa take 4-7 years to flower.

Veratrum seedlings develop slowly and take years to flower.

Wisteria take many years to flower.

Zantedeschia flower in 2-3 years.

ANNUALS

An annual is a plant that naturally germinates, sets seed and dies within one growing season.

BIENNIALS

Biennials produce foliage in their first year, in the second year they flower, set seed and die.

PERENNIALS

Perennials can be short-lived and some are grown as annuals. However, most perennials are long-lived plants. The term strictly applies to plants that make growth for three years or more.

QUICK FLOWERING PLANTS

Perennials are known to be slower from seed and in general when propagated, but here are some from seed which will not keep you waiting for flowers. The selection of perennials and biennials given below will flower from their first year from an early sowing.

Abutilon
Achillea
Agastache
Alcea
Asarina
Asclepias
Begonia semperflorens
Begonia tuberous
Belamcanda chinensis
Brugmansia
Buddleja
Buphthalmum
Calceolaria
Campanula carpatica
Campanula cochlearifolia
Canna
Catananche
Chrysanthemum indicum
Clematis some spp
Clitoria
Cobaea
Commelina
Coreopsis
Datura
Delosperma
Delphinium
Dianthus caryophyllus
Dianthus spp (pinks)
Eccremocarpus
Echinacea
Eupatorium
Gaillardia
Gaura
Geum
Heliotropium
Heterotheca
Knautia
Kniphofia miniature hybrids
Lavandula multifida

Limonium
Lobelia 'Queen Victoria'
Linum
Lupinus
Lychnis
Malva
Mimulus
Monarda
Myosotis
Nepeta
Nierembergia
Oenothera
Papaver
Pelargonium bedding types
Penstemon
Rosa polyanthus
Salvia some spp
Sphaeralcea incana
Streptocarpus
Symphyandra
Tanacetum
Trachelium some
Tropaeolum peregrinum
Verbena bonariensis

GROWING TIP

The first buds of Meconopsis betonicifolia are best picked off . If the plant is prevented from flowering until several crowns have formed, it will be less likely to be short-lived.

MONOCARPIC plants flower once and die. These include some Meconopsis species and Cardiocrinum which takes about 7 years to flower from seed and then dies after flowering, leaving many offsets.

SELF-SEEDERS

Once you have sown the following, you will never be without them. This can often be a great advantage because you are getting more plants for free. However, with some prolific self-seeders, it can become the reverse. If you do not want the plants to seed themselves everywhere, dead-head after flowering.

Some plants are fickle and only self-seed when they are in the perfect spot. Others quickly become a nuisance everywhere, so you have been warned. If you are not sure how a self-seeder will behave, remove flowers as soon as they fade, you can still dry seed pods indoors and use the seed to sow at the appropiate time. Or select a few pods to leave and ripen on the stems and sow into your garden. Remember some seed-heads contain hundreds of seeds.

Aethionema grandiflorum especially on raised beds
Aethionema saxatile especially on raised beds
Agrostemma spp
Alchemilla most spp especially A. mollis
Anemone 'Leeds Variety'
Anemone pavoniana
Anthericum liliago
Anthriscus cerefolium
Aquilegia spp
Argemone may
Aruncus spp
Asarum some spp
Aster novae-belgii
Athyrium filix-femina on moist, peaty ground
Blumenbachia hieronymi
Borago laxiflora
Borago pygmaea
Briza spp
Calendula spp
Camassia
Campanula barbata
Campanula latifolia
Campanula rotundifolia
Chelidonium spp
Chionodoxa
Corydalis lutea
Corydalis ochroleuca
Crepis spp

Crocus many spp
Dicentra formosa 'Bountiful'
Dicentra hybrids
Dicksonia antartica in Cornwall and west coast of Ireland
Dicranostigma spp
Dierama spp
Digitalis with ease
Dryopteris filix-mas freely on moist, peaty ground
Eranthis
Erigeron philadelphicus
Erinus alpinus
Erodium manescaui
Eschscholzia spp
Euphorbia dulcis
Foeniculum vulgare
Fritillaria pyrenaica
Gagea lutea
Gagea villosa
Galtonia, when suited
Geranium most spp too freely
Geranium phaeum mildly
Geranium sinense sparingly
Geranium versicolor
Gladiolus byzantinus on light soil only
Hacquetia epipactis
Helleborus orientalis on retentive soil
Heracleum mantegazzianum
Hieracium lanatum sometimes
Hieracium spp
Holcus mollis 'Variegatus'

Hyacinthoides spp
Hyoscyamus spp
Ionopsidium spp
Isatis spp
Kniphofia spp varied results
Linaria spp especially L. purpurea
Lobelia bedding types in
suitable climates
Luma apiculata may
Lupinus polyphyllus
Lysichitum freely when established
Lythrum spp
Macleaya spp
Malva spp
Meconopsis cambrica
Melissa officinalis ('Variegata'
will revert)
Michauxia may
Milium effusum 'Aureum' mildly
Mitella spp
Myosotis with ease
Myrrhis odorata
Narcissus
Nectaroscordum
Nemophila
Nepeta spp
Nicandra physalodes
Nigella
Oenothera glazioviana prolifically
Ornithogalum
Paeonia veitchii
Paeonia veitchii woodwardii
Papaver
Phytolacca spp
Plantago spp
Rumex spp
Sarcocapnos often under glass
Scilla spp especially S. autumnale
Silene monachorum
Sisyrinchium
Solidago
Spartium may
Stipa arundinacea not in cold areas,
but seeds itself in heavy soils in
Yorkshire.
Tanacetum parthenium freely
Thlaspi may

Tulipa sprengeri in a shady damp
position in acid, sandy soil.
Verbascum phoeniceum
Verbena bonariensis freely in
warmer counties

SHY SEEDERS

By contrast the following are very shy of setting seed, or produce no seed at all or little viable seed.

Anthericum major
Bolax
Brachyscome
Celmisia
Epimedium spp
Gazania rigens
Helleborus atrorubens in cultivation
Musa and Ensete spp
Strophanthus spp
Stylophorum diphyllum
Tagetes Zenith Series do not produce seed.

SETTING SEED

Some plants set seed prolifically anywhere, others only set seed under prime conditions. Some species do not set seed every year.

Although you can obtain seed of some double flowers, such as Meconopsis cambrica flore pleno, many double-flowered types are self-sterile and do not produce seed.

The hemp agrimony is a weed in Britain, but the double-flowered form Eupatorium cannabinum 'Flore Pleno' is quite desirable as it does not seed itself.

Annuals and Biennials

These are usually prolific seeders, producing large quantities of seed to ensure survival.

SAVING SEED

Seed is usually worth saving from plants in your garden. For vegetables you need to observe the spacings required to avoid cross-pollination and obtain seed that is true to type.

Seed from F1's is not normally worth saving, you can still save and sow this seed, but you will most likely obtain plants inferior to those with which you started. Most F1's are unnecessary to the home gardener, they were developed for commercial suppliers, diversity should be more important than uniformity in our gardens. Cross-pollinated plants may provide some unusual variations from seed, you may be lucky and come up with something entirely different. Self-pollinating plants will usually come true.

Seed collecting

This, like seed sowing, is an ongoing process. Some plants drop their seed really quickly so you must be vigilant. Others seed over a long time. I collected seed of Geranium maderense in my garden over a period of many weeks. You can collect seed in plastic bags, but these are no good for storage. Better to use paper bags for collection. In some cases, you need to cover the seed head with a bag and collect seed in this way or it will be dispersed far and wide before you have a chance to collect it.

To save seed be ready as soon as the pods ripen, many pods change colour at this point. Choose a dry, warm day if possible. You have a choice of cutting off the seed heads and drying them on trays on a sunny windowsill or in a greenhouse. They can also be hung upside down with paper bags attached to catch the seed. Alternatively, you can collect the seed straight from the plant, again by attaching paper bags to seed heads, or cellophane bags if rain is imminent. Or collect small amounts each day as the seed ripens. This is virtually impossible for large amounts of seed, but does have the advantage of the seed ripening on the plant.

Storing seed

Most seed you have collected or that which you have purchased will remain viable for some time if you store it correctly. Open seed packets are often left in warm rooms or in the greenhouse and will quickly deteriorate if left in these conditions. To maximise the life of seed you must never store in high temperatures or high humidity. Even seed sold in metal foil packets are subject to the same deterioration once opened.

HOW TO STORE SEED

Seal packets firmly. Place into a screw-top glass jar. Alternativley, use an empty film case. Enclose a small sachet of silica gel. Place the container in a refrigerator.

VIABILITY

Viability is how long the seed will give optimum germination. This can vary immensely. Some seeds are still viable over 100 years, others are just viable for up to 3 days. The following tables give the average shelf-life of a number of genera provided they are stored as recommended on the previous page.

Acca 1 year +
Aeonium very short
Andropogon 3-4 years
Anethum 3-5 years
Anigozanthos 10 years
Annona 5 years
Antirrhinum 3-7 years
Aquilegia 5 years
Armeria 3 years
Artemisia 3-9 years
Asperula 3 years
Atriplex 6 years
Bauhinia 1 year +
Bellis 6-7 years
Borago 8-10 yeas
Brassica 4-15 years
Briza 3 years
Calomeria short viability
Carum 3-5 years
Cassia 158 years
Casuarina 12 years +
Celosia 4-8 years
Centaurea 5-10 years
Centranthus 4 years
Cerastium 4-7 years
Cercocarpus 5 years
Chrysanthemum 1-10 years
Clematis 1-3 years
Cobaea 2 years +
Coix 3 years
Convolvulus 26 years
Coreopsis 6-8 years
Cosmos 6 years
Crassula tend to be short-lived
Cuminum 3 yeas
Cupressus 20 years
Dianthus 5-10 years
Dolichos 4-10 years

Echinops 2 years+
Erysimum cheiri 3-5 years
Grevillea 4 years
Haworthia 6 months
Helenium 3-4 years
Heliotropium 50 years
Kalanchoe sometimes has very poor viabilty
Lotus up to 100 years
Lunaria 4 years
Lychnis 3-4 years
Malva up to 200 years
Matricaria 2-3 years
Momordica 3-4 years
Nepeta 5 years
Osmunda lose viability quickly, sow within 3 days of ripening.
Paulownia 4 years
Penstemon 8-16 years
Persicaria up to 25 years
Petrorhagia saxifraga 10 years
Petunia 8-16 years
Phytolacca 40 years
Polygonum up to 25 years
Portulaca 3-10 years, some up to 45
Primula 1-5 years
Primula veris 2-5 years
Ricinus 25 years
Rumex up to 80 years
Salvia azurea 5 years
Salvia viridis 15 years
Schizanthus 20 years
Sedum 3-5 years
Tanacetum 3 years
Tropaeolum 5 years
Verbena 2-14 years
Viola 2-12 years
Yucca 6 years +

VIABILITY OF VEGETABLES AND HERBS

Amaranth 5 years
Angelica 3 months
Artichoke 5 years
Asparagus 3-5 years
Asparagus pea 2 years
Aubergine 5 years
Basil 5 years
Beet 5 years
Beetroot 5 years
Borage 5 years
Broad bean 3 years
Broccoli 5 years
Brussel sprouts 4 years
Cabbage 4 years
Cape gooseberry 3 years
Cardoon 4 years
Carrot 3 years
Cauliflower 4 years
Celeriac 5 years
Celery 5 years
Chervil 1 year
Chicory 8 years
Chinese cabbage 5 years
Chives 1 year
Coriander 6 years
Corn 2-10 years
Corn salad 5 years
Courgette 3-10 years
Cress, garden 5 years
Cucumber 4-10 years
Dill 3 years
Endive 5 years
Fennel 4 years
Fenugreek 4 years +
French bean 3 years
Garlic chives 1 year
Kale 4 years
Kohl rabi 4 years
Leek 3 years
Lettuce 6 years
Marjoram 5 years
Marrow 3-10 years
Melon 5 years
Mint 1 year
Mitsuba 3 years

Mizuna 2 years
Mustard 3-7 years
Mustard greens 4 years
New Zealand spinach 6 years
Okra 5 years
Onion 2 years
Orach 5 years
Parsley 2 years
Parsnip maximum 1 year
Pea 3 years
Pepper 5 years
Pumpkin 3-10 years
Radish 4 years
Rhubarb 1 year
Rocket 2 years
Rosemary 1 year
Rue 2 years
Runner bean 3 years
Sage 3 years
Salad burnet 3 years
Salsify 3-5 years
Scorzonera 3-5 years
Shungiku 3 years
Silver beet 10 years
Sorrel 3 years
Soya bean 3 years
Spinach 5 years
Squash 3-10 years
Swede 4 years
Swiss chard 4 years
Thyme 2-7 years
Tomato 5 years
Turnip 4 years
Watercress 5 years
Watermelon 5 years
Welsh onion 2 years

TESTING VIABILITY

Place seeds in hot water in a jar. Seed which sinks is more likely to be viable. Test the germination rate by sowing a percentage of seeds. Depending on how many germinate, you can then decide if you wish to go ahead and sow.

SEED FORMATION

Plants can be self or cross-pollinated. Many animals are busy day and night pollinating plants. Once pollinated the plant produces seed, as a means of survival. Some plants do not produce seed or produce so little that they are propagated vegetatively.

PROPAGATING PLANTS FROM SEED

Seed is a sexual means of reproduction. The seed is the basic biological unit for the reproduction of conifers (gymnosperms) and flowering plants (angiosperms).

Each seed combines male and female genes in a plant embryo and gives rise to offspring that varies genetically from the parent plant. In this way, the species preserves and perpetuates its identity, yet constantly evolves and adapts to changes in the environment.

Seeds are capable of colonizing vast areas. They can lie dormant for many years, waiting for the right conditions to germinate so that they can maximise the chances of survival. This is typical of cacti in the desert, which can lie dormant for years until the periodic rains come, bringing them to life.

Flower structure

In flowering plants, the process of seed production begins in the flower itself. Some species bear male and female flowers on separate plants. However, in most species they are borne on the same plant. Flowers are extremely diverse, but most are composed of inner petals and outer sepals, collectively known as tepals or outer perianth segments.

The female reproductive part of the flower is the ovary. It is here the seeds are produced. The style, a slender stalk, connects the ovary with the stigma, the receptor of pollen. Together, ovary, style and stigma form the carpel. There may be one or several carpels, always situated at the centre or apex of the flower. Each stamen has a slender filament which supports the anther, where pollen is produced.

Begonias are monoecious, they have separate male and female flowers on the same plant. Schlumbergera are bisexual, they have both stigma and stamens. Some flowers are single-sexed and have only stamens or carpels. Dioecious species, such as Ilex and Skimmia, have male and female flowers on separate plants and they must be grown together to obtain fruits which carry seeds. It may be impossible to tell the sex of seed-grown dioecious plants for many years.

Pollination

A flower must first be pollinated before it can produce seed. Pollination is the process of transferring the male pollen from the anther to the female stigma. Plants can be pollinated in two ways.

A plant can be self-pollinating, thereby reducing the genetic variation of the species. Many wild species have systems to prevent self-pollination.

Other plants are cross-pollinated in several diverse ways. We all know bees pollinate plants. So too do wasps, other flying creatures including moths and bats at night and the wind also plays an important part. The male flowers of Sweetcorn are grouped at the top of the plant to catch the wind and ensure pollen is blown onto the stigmas of the female flowers lower down the plant. Water is also used in pollination.

The ingenuity of plants

Nature should never be under-estimated and plants use every trick in the book to ensure pollination, setting of seed and survival.

To ensure cross-pollination, plants have developed a wide range of interesting techniques. They exploit insects or animals to transfer the pollen to the stigma. We might find the colour and spectacular flowers of some species beautiful and irrestible, but they are not there to look pretty for us, their purpose is to attract a pollinator.

We might inhale their sweet perfume, but this is nothing more than another way to catch the attention of flying insects and animals. Pollinators are rewarded with nectar or pollen.

Some orchids are shaped and smell like female insects to lure males to mate with them. Some flowers, such as Stapelia, have the smell of rotting-flesh to attract flies. Pollinators include bats, beetles, butterflies, flies, moths and small mammals.

The developing seed

Pollen has to be compatible and alive. The stigma must be receptive, usually exuding a sticky, sugary solution. In this way, the pollen sticks easily and if compatible, the pollen forms a pollen tube. The tube burrows down the style so that the male sex cells can enter the ovary and fertilize the female egg cell, the ovule.

The male and female cells contain chromosomes which hold genetic material from each parent plant. Seed begins to form when a male sex cell fuses with the single egg nucleus and a full set of chromosomes is realised.

Seed structure

A fully developed seed consists of an embryo - a tiny plant with a shoot (plumule) and a root (radicle), together with seed leaves (cotyledons), all surrounded by a store of food (endosperm). In angiosperms, the endosperm develops before the embryo, but in most gymnosperms, the embryo forms first. An outer layer - the seed coat (testa) - protects the embryo and its food store from attack by bacteria, fungi, insects or animals as well as environmental factors such as drought, flooding or wildly varying temperatures. The maturing seed often dries on the plant. Achieving the correct dryness is thought to affect the capacity of the seed to germinate. Some seeds are as fine as dust and generally produced in thousands by as little as one plant, others such as Lodoicea are as big as footballs. Seeds are usually enclosed in protective casings.

Unlike angiosperms, the 'naked' seed of gymnosperms such as Conifers, Cycads or Ginkgo biloba are enclosed only partly by tissues of the parent plant. Conifer cones are wind-pollinated and seeds are formed on the female cones.

Plants such as ferns, liverworts, mosses and horsetail reproduce by spores. These may look like seed, but are asexual and develop male and female sex organs independently from the plant that bore it. The sexual stage of reproduction can occur in the presence of water.

Seed dispersal

Once formed and ripened, the seeds disperse. Seeds can be dispersed by the wind or by animals. Some burst explosively to disperse the seeds far and wide. Some seeds will germinate as soon as ripe while still on the parent plant. These include grasses, cereals and amaryllis bulbs.

Ecballium elaterium has earned its name of squirting cucumber, its pods are filled with a watery liquid which bursts under pressure, expelling a stream of seeds and juice into the air. So do not stand too close to ripening pods!

HOW A SEED GERMINATES

There are two basic ways in which a seed germinates. The two methods are known as hypogeal and epigeal germination.

Fresh seed will germinate rapidly. However, most seed available commercially is dried. For a dried seed to germinate it needs water which causes it to swell. Most seeds double in size before germinating. This is obvious when you pre-soak seeds. The seed embryo needs oxygen. You must also provide the correct temperature which varies considerably so refer to the table. Germination can be delayed by a too high or too low temperature. Some seeds need light. There are two basic ways in which seeds germinate, hypogeal and epigeal. Once germinated if the correct conditions are not given, as to light, moisture and warmth, a seedling can soon die.

Epigeal germination

Plants such as the tomato (Lycopersicon) and beech (Fagus) emerge by elevating the seed leaves above the surface at the same time as the root (radicle) develops, this is known as epigeal germination. If the shoot tip is frosted or killed, the plant can grow no further.

Hypogeal germination

Hypogeal germination occurs with plants such as the pea (Pisum) or oak (Quercus) and some bulbs, when the seed leaves and food store remain in the soil with the root. The growing shoot emerges only when the true leaves form. If the seed is deep enough, it has a good chance of survival if the shoot tip is damaged as it is able to produce secondary shoots. It may be many months before any sign of growth is seen by the gardener when hypogeal germination is taking place beneath the soil.

GERMINATION OF SEED

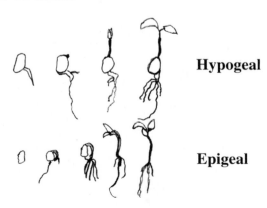

Hypogeal

Epigeal

POLLINATION

Plants are self or cross pollinated. Cross-pollinated plants are pollinated by a variety of insects or small animals or by wind.

The tables given below will help you distinguish whether herbs and vegetables are self or cross-pollinated. Some are both.

CROSS-POLLINATED

Amaranth
Artichoke
Asparagus
Aubergine
Basil
Beetroot
Borage
Broad bean
Broccoli
Brussel Sprouts
Cabbage
Cardoon
Carrot
Cauliflower
Celeriac
Celery
Chervil
Chicory
Chinese cabbage
Chives
Coriander
Corn
Corn salad
Cucumber
Dill
Fennel
Garlic chives
Jerusalem artichoke
Kale
Kohlrabi
Leek
Marjoram
Marrow
Melon
Mint
Mitsuba
Mizuna
Mustard

Mustard greens
Nasturtium
New Zealand spinach
Okra
Onion
Orach
Parsley
Parsnip
Pepper
Pumpkin
Radish
Rhubarb
Rocket
Rosemary
Sage
Salad burnet
Salsify
Scorzonera
Shungiku
Silver beet
Sorrel
Spinach
Squash
Sunflower
Thyme
Turnip
Watermelon
Welsh onion

Aubergine, Broad bean and Pepper can also self-pollinate.

HAND-POLLINATION

A useful method of ensuring pollination if there are no insects or other pollinators around, or if you wish to be sure of the parents involved and wish to control pollination.

SELF-POLLINATED

Asparagus pea
Aubergine
Broad bean
Cape gooseberry
Endive
French bean
Lettuce
Pea
Pepper
Runner bean
Tomato
Watercress

INSECT-POLLINATED

Most species, including vegetables are insect-pollinated. Plants which have a sweet evening or night scent and whose flowers open at night, such as Oenothera, evening primrose, are normally pollinated by moths.

There are some flowers with a particular strange kind of beauty such as Amorphophallus and Stapelias which have a smell you would not want to get too close to, but this is to attract their pollinators, flies.

Beetles are attracted to brightly coloured flowers such as the large yellow blooms of Luffa aegyptica, the loofah.

Bats, especially in warm climates, are attracted by nectar-producing flowers, such as the night-blooming Cactus species, Cereus. Again, the scent is not that pleasant, the bats are attracted by the powerful, foul-smelling odour. The bat transfers pollen onto other flowers from its fur.

Butterflies are attracted to many flowering plants such as Buddleja, known as the butterfly bush and Echinacea the coneflower. You can even purchase seed mixtures of plants which will attract butterflies to your garden. Believe it or not a patch of nettles will be advantageous.

The Queen of all pollinators has to be the bee. Again there are definite bee plants which will attract bees to your garden. Watch a bee performing its miracle of pollination and you will be fascinated by the pollen sticking to this busy creature as they go from plant to plant.

WIND-POLLINATED

A number of flowers and vegetables are also pollinated by wind. These include the following:
Amaranth
Beetroot
Corn
Orach
Silver beet
Spinach

Both Beetroot and Corn are also pollinated by insects.

HYBRIDIZATION

A hybrid is a cross between two different plants. The cross can occur between two selections of the same plant or between two species, and occasionally between two different genera.

The exchange of genetic material in plants, by the sexual production of seed, is fundamental to the evolvement of the plant and its ability to adapt to environmental changes and ensure survival. This ability has been exploited by breeders to produce new hybrids which are designed to offer us improved colour or form, habit, disease-resistance or scent. I myself prefer open-pollinated varieties over F1 hybrids.

Some plants hybridise very easily on their own, without any help. Others are produced intentionally. In commercial hybridizing, parents are carefully chosen for their characteristics. They need to be stable and to breed true. One parent is chosen as the seed (female) and the other as the pollen (male) parent. Flowers on the female have their stamens removed as soon as possible to avoid self-pollination. They are then hand-pollinated with the male parent. The seed parent is covered with a muslin bag so that accidental insect-pollination is impossible.

F1 hybrids, the first generation, are uniform and tend to flower at the same time, they are also expensive to buy. A second generation is sometimes produced - the F2 hybrids.

Creating your own hybrids

This is part of the fun of growing from seed. Many species lend themselves to hybridizing on an amateur scale, and it is not too difficult to produce pleasing offspring. Try to concentrate on one species, you will need a methodical approach and a good deal of patience. Select parents and commence hybridizing. be selective, you will need to throw a great many seedlings away.

A small fine paintbrush is useful for transferring pollen, a pair of tweezers, and fine, sharp scissors a fine net or muslin to protect the female from further accidental pollination, and a notebook to record your crosses. Write down the name and characteristics of your chosen parents and the resultant crosses.

It helps to have a specific aim, such as breeding a hardier range of Kniphofias, or introducing a new colour.

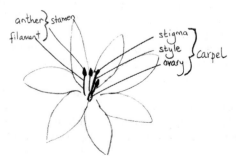

HYBRIDIZE EASILY

There are a number of genera which hybridize easily. The ones in the following list may hybridize naturally in the garden and may not therefore produce plants typical of the parent when grown from seed. Most of them will however produce pleasant and interesting plants.

Althaea
Amelanchier
Anthemis sancti-johannis
Aquilegia
Berberis
Bergenia
Betula
Ceanothus
Celmisia
Eremurus
Erysimum
Eucalyptus
Galanthus
Geranium endressii
Geranium versicolor
Hyacinthoides
Hyperican may
Iris
Nothofagus
Primula waltonii
Pulmonaria
Rhododendron
Tilia
Tulipa
Weigela

Begonia
Dahlia
Erysimum
Hosta
Hemerocallis
Iris
Lewisia
Lilium
Rosa
Tagetes

Experiment with hybrids

The following are a good choice for experimenting with your own hybrids. The challenge of producing something new can lead to an interesting and exciting hobby.

Some seed companies and nurseries are always interested in something new and different. One seed catalogue already features several seeds which have been raised by their customers.

Good hybrids must be stable and come true from seed. Seed companies may be willing to perform trials on the hybrids you produce to assess their suitability for release.

Anthemis sanct-johannis often hybridizes with A, tinctoria and thereby loses its rich, orange colour.

Geranium versicolor hybridizes with G.endressii and is perhaps better not introduced into the gardens, but left as a wild plant.

Pulmonarias cross-fertilize easily and produce variable plants.

Garden-collected seed of Tilia will yield variable hybrids.

Garden seed of Rhododendron will not generally come true, but that of wild-collected seed and hand-pollinated garden plants produce plants that are true to type.

TRUE FROM SEED

Sometimes seed is available from plants which will not come true. Bear in mind that in general seed of cultivars does not come true, but seed of species does come true.

Here is a selective list of plants I have found which come true from seed. They may not all come 100% true and some will only struggle to about 50%, so be selective. Discard any green seedlings of variegated seeds, choose your time to do this. Variegation does not always show from the start on seedlings. On Lunaria annua variegated form, the variegation may not show until the flowering time of the species.

Many variegated plants need to be propagated by division and are not always reliable from seed. Selection is of most importance with coloured leaves, especially purple leaves, the colour can be poor from seed, so select the very best. Remember just because a seed is on sale does not mean it will breed true. Only cultivars propagated vegetatively can bear the cultivar name.

Aconitum carmichaelii Wilsonii Group 'Barker's Variety'
Aesculus x carnea
Alcea 'Arabian Nights'
Alcea 'Blackcurrant Whirl'
Anthriscus sylvestris 'Ravenswing'
Aquilegia 'Ballerina'
Aquilegia clematiflora 'Green Apples'
Aquilegia 'Iceberg'
Aquilegia 'Mellow Yellow'
Aquilegia 'Roman Bronze'
Aquilegia 'Royal Purple'
Aquilegia 'Silver Edge'
Aquilegia 'Sunburst Ruby'
Aquilegia vulgaris 'Nivea'
Aquilegia vulgaris 'Nora Barlow'
Aquilegia vulgaris Vervaeneana Group
Aquilegia 'William Guiness'
Arabis blepharophylla 'Fruhlingszauber'
Astilbe taquetii 'Superba'
Astrantia involucrata 'Shaggy'
Astrantia major 'Ruby Wedding Series'
Barbarea vulgaria 'Variegata'
Campanula 'Faichem Lilac'
Campanula lactiflora 'Pritchard's Variety'
Carex comans 'Frosted Curls'
Cotoneaster spp some

Dianthus barbatus 'Sooty'
Digitalis cultivars
Digitalis x mertonensis
Echinacea purpurea 'White Star'
Eryngium giganteum (Miss Willmott's Ghost)
Erysimum 'Ellen Willmott'
Euphorbia dulcis 'Chameleon'
Euphorbia griffithii 'Fireglow'
Fritillaria some
Gentiana asclepiadea some pale-blue hybrids
Geranium clarkei 'Kashmir Purple'
Geranium macrorhizum 'Bevan's Variety'
Geranium phaeum 'Lily Lovell'
Geranium phaeum 'Samobor'
Geranium pratense 'Rose Queen'
Geranium pyrenaicum 'Bill Wallis'
Geranium robertianum 'Celtic White'
Geranium sylvaticum 'Albiflorum'
Geranium wallichianum 'Buxton's Variety'
Geranium x oxonianum 'Claridge Druce'
Geum 'Lady Stratheden'
Geum 'Mrs. Bradshaw'
Haloragis 'Wellington Bronze'
Helleborus orientalis olympicus

Helleborus 'Wester Flisk'
Heuchera 'Emperor's Cloak'
Heuchera 'Greenfinch'
Heuchera macrantha v diversifolia 'Palace Purple'
Hosta elegans
Hosta sieboldiana
Hosta ventricosa
Humulus japonicus 'Variegatus'
Hypericum androsaemum 'Gladis Brabazon'
Lathyrus latifolius 'Red Pearl'
Lathyrus latifolius 'White Pearl'
Lathyrus odoratus spp
Lavatera arborea 'Variegata'
Ligularia dentata 'Desdemona'
Ligularia dentata 'Othello'
Lupinus
Maurandya 'Red Dragon'
Meconopsis cambrica 'Frances Perry'
Meconopsis cambrica 'Muriel Brown'
Melissa officinalis 'Allgold'
Milium effusum 'Aureum'
Nepeta 'Six Hills Giant'
Nicotiana langsdorfii 'Cream-Splash'
Oenothera 'Sunset Boulevard'
Penstemon
Persicaria virginiana variegated
Phormium tenax 'Purpureum'
Polemonium 'Apricot Delight'
Potentilla 'Etna'
Potentilla nepalensis 'Miss Willmott'
Potentilla nepalensis 'Roxana'
Primula japonica 'Millar's Crimson'
Primula japonica 'Postford White'
Ranunculua acris 'Citrinus'
Rheum palmatum atrosanguineum
Salvia meryame 'Mint Suace'
Sidalcea candida
Sidalcea 'Croftway Red'
Silene 'Graham's Delight'
Symphytum variegated forms
Verbascum 'Pink Domino'
Viola 'Bowles' Black'
Viola 'Fuji Dawn'
Viola 'Green Jade'
Viola 'Rodney Davey'

SEED-RAISED PLANTS
The following have been raised from seed.

Abies alba 'Pendula' as a seedling in France in 1835.

Agapanthus 'Headbourne Hybrids'

Aster x frikartii raised by Frikart in Switzerland, 'Monch' is by far the best.

Bergenia 'Sunningdale'

Euphorbia griffithii 'Dixter' selected by Christopher Lloyd from seedlings.

Forms of Thalictrum aquilegiifolium

Geranium 'Johnson's Blue' originated from seed of G.pratense sent by A.T. Johnson to Mr. B.Ruys of Dedemsvaart.

Ginkgo biloba 'Tremonia' a columnar form raised as a seedling in Dortmund Botanic Garden in 1930.

Hedychium coccineum 'Stephen' from seed collected by A.D. Schilling.

Heuchera micrantha diversifolia 'Palace Purple' from wild collected seeds at Kew by Brian Halliwell.

Impatiens 'Spectra' new Guinea Group.

In Japan, the name Benibana, given to forms of Styrax japonica with pink flowers which are raised from seed.

Juniperus 'Columnaris Glauca' a seedling selected by the U.S. Department of Agriculture from seed collected by Frank N.Meyer in Hubei.

Kniphofia 'Green Jade' was raised from seed from the garden of Sir Cedric Morris, Suffolk, by Beth Chatto.

Pseudotsuga menziesii 'Fletcheri' originated as a seedling on P. menziesii v glauca in 1906, as did P. menziesii 'Nana'.

Santolina rosmariniifolia 'Primrose Gem' originated as a seedling at Hilliers pre-1960.

Sorbus 'Edwin Hillier' - the mother plant was raised at Hilliers nursery.

SEEDS TO THE GRAM

A useful indication of how many seeds you need to sow is the quantity of seed per gram. Some seeds are like fine dust, others are large and easy to handle. It gives a good indication of the size of the seed.

Achillea filipendula 1000
Actaea 40
Actaea pachypoda 40
Adenophora 500
Adlumia fungosa 70
Agastache 500
Alcea rosea 40
Alchemilla mollis 1000
Allium cristophii 60
Allium fistulosum 150
Alonsoa 3400
Althaea officinalis 40
Alyssoides 100
Amaranth 800
Amsonia 60
Anacyclus depressus 500
Anchusa 60
Andropogon 100
Anemone most 200
Anthemis 500
Anthoxanthum 200
Anthyllis 350
Antirrhinum 6000
Aquilegia most 150 - 200
Arabis blepharophylla 500
Arabis caucasica 1000
Arctotis 200
Arenaria 1000
Arisaema triphyllum 12
Artichoke 30
Aruncus dioicus 1000
Asarina 350
Asclepias 50
Asparagus 50
Asparagus pea 18
Asperula 600
Aster alpinus 700
Aster bigelovii 2000
Astilbe spp 2000
Aubergine 200
Aurinia saxatilis 300

Baptisia australis 30
Basil 600
Bean, French 3
Bean, runner 3
Beetroot 50
Bellis 1000
Bergenia 1000
Berlandiera 150
Bidens 600
Borage 65
Bouteloua 250
Broad bean 1
Broccoli 300
Bromus 100
Brussel sprouts 270
Buphthalmum 1100
Cabbage 250
Calamintha 3000
Calendula 150
Campanula most 500
Campanula carpatica 1500
Canna 5
Cape gooseberry 400
Cardoon 25
Carex 330
Carrot 1000
Catananche 500
Cauliflower 500
Celeriac 2000
Celery 2000
Centaurea macrocephala 25
Cephalaria 25
Cerinthe major 25
Chaenorrhinum 10000
Chervil 450
Chicory 600
Chinese cabbage 350
Chives 600
Cimicifuga racemosa 200
Cimicifuga ramosa 400
Clematis integrifolia 100

Clematis orientalis 200
Codonopsis 500
Coreopsis 125
Coriander 90
Corn 5
Corn salad 700
Corydalis 200
Corynephorus 1000
Cucumber 40
Cuphea 275
Datura meteloides 25
Delphinium most 200
Dianthus barbatus 500
Dianthus deltoides 1000
Dianthus knappii 300
Dictamnus albus 13
Digitalis grandiflora 1000
Digitalis pupurea 2000
Dill 900
Dimorphotheca 450
Dipsacus 100
Dodecatheon 500
Draba 750
Eccremocarpus 250
Echinacea purpurea 100
Endive 900
Eragrostis 330
Erodium 150
Eryngium 90
Erysimum allioni 300
Eupatorium 500
Euphorbia polycroma 100
Fennel 500
Festuca ovina glauca 330
Fibigia clypeata 125
Gaillardia 80
Galega 50
Garlic 7
Garlic chives 250
Gaura 50
Geranium 150
Geum borisii 200
Geum 'Lady Stratheden' 300
Geum triflorum 350
Glaucium flavum 350
Gypsophila 350
Helenium autumnale 1000

Helenium hoopesii 200
Heliopsis 100
Hesperis 100
Heuchera 'Greenfinch' 2000
Hosta sieboldiana 100
Hypericum 1000
Hyssopus 850
Hystrix 50
Iberis sempervirens 250
Incarvillea sinensis 250
Inula 200
Iris chrysographes 35
Iris pseudacorus 10
Iris setosa 35
Isatis tinctoria 25
Kale 250
Kitaibelia 330
Knautia macedonica 250
Koeleria glauca 330
Kohl rabi 250
Lathyrus heterophyllus 15
Lathyrus latifolius 25
Lathyrus laxiflorus 75
Lathyrus linifolius 70
Lathyrus montanus 70
Lathyrus nervosus 39
Lathyrus niger 37
Lathyrus odoratus 12-15
Lathyrus palustris 17
Lathyrus pratensis 110
Lathyrus sylvestris 20
Lathyrus tuberosus 25
Lathyrus vernus 80
Laurentia axillaris 12000
Lavandula multifida 1000
Lavandula viridis 800
Lavatera thuringiaca 40
Leek 400
Lettuce 1000
Leucanthemum x superbum 750
Lilium 35
Linum 100
Lobelia cardinalis 2000
Lobelia inflata 2500
Lunaria annua 15
Lupinus arboreus 8
Lupinus polyphyllus 25

Lychnis chalcedonica 1000
Lychnis flos-cuculi 2200
Macleaya cordata 500
Malope 300
Malva moschata 100
Malva sylvestris 175
Marjoram 12000
Marrow 7
Marrubium 1000
Melica altissima 200
Melica ciliata 1000
Melon 30
Mint 40000
Mitsuba 500
Mizuna 600
Monarda didyma 330
Mustard 600
Myosotis alpestris 1200
Myrrhis odorata 20
Nemesia 5000
Nepeta most 330
New Zealand spinach 20
Nicandra 1000
Nicotiana most 2000
Nicotiana sylvestris 1000
Oenothera biennis 200
Okra 15
Onion 250
Onopordum 25
Opuntia 25
Orach 250
Oxyria 500
Panicum 200
Papaver orientale 750
Papaver rhoeas 3500
Papaver somniferum 1000
Parsley 200
Parsnip 200
Parthenocissus 35
Pea 5
Penstemon most 500
Pepper 150
Petunia 9000
Phlomis 65
Phuopsis 330
Platycodon 330
Poa alpina 1000

Polemonium 330
Potentilla 1000
Primula polyanthus 500
Primula veris 200
Pulsatilla 200
Pumpkin 4
Radish 100
Ratibida 200
Rhubarb 250
Rocket 500
Rosemary 900
Rudbeckia 330
Runner bean 1
Sage 250
Salad burnet 150
Salsify 100
Salvia sclarea 250
Sanguisorba 200
Sarracenia 500
Schizachryium 100
Schizanthus 1600
Scorzonera 100
Sedum 4000
Shungiku 300
Sidalcea 100
Silene dioica 500
Silver beet 75
Silybum 35
Sisymbrium 200
Sisyrinchium 200
Sitanon 330
Sorghastrum 100
Sorrel 1000
Soya bean 7
Spinach 70
Spodiopogon 330
Stachys byzantina 200
Swede 150
Symphyandra 500
Tagetes 1100
Tanacetum parthenium 500
Thermopsis 50
Thyme 1000
Tomato 400
Turnip 300
Watermelon 6
Welsh onion 250

EDIBLE SEEDS

Most of us eat and enjoy nuts, unless we are unfortunate enough to be allergic to them, and maybe some of us have been adventurous enough to eat Nasturtium seed, but did you know just how many edible seeds there are?

Take a look at the list below and I think you will be pleasantly surprised. Many seeds have excellent protein content too. Seed pods and some kernels are also edible. Many seeds are also nutritious if sprouted.

Abelmoschus
Acacia retinodes
Acacia suaveolens
Acanthosicyos horridus
Acrocomia mexicana kernel
Acrocomia totai kernel
Adansonia digitata
Adansonia gregorii
Adenanthera pavonina
Agastache urticifolia
Aleurites molucanna
Allium sativum
Aloe vera
Amaranthus dubius
Amaranthus graecizans
Amaranthus hybridus
Amaranthus hypochondriacus
Amphicaroaea monoica
Anacolosa luzoniensis
Apios americana
Araucaria
Arundinaria
Balanties aegyptiaca
Balsamorhiza deltoidea
Bambusa
Bauhinia racemosa
Bauhinia tomentosa
Benincasa
Benincasa hispida
Bertholletia excelsa
Bischofia javanica
Bixa orellana
Bombax ellipticum white forms
Boscia albitrunca
Boswellia serrata
Brachychiton diversifolium

Bromus carinatus
Buchanania lanzan
Caesalpinia pulcherrima
Cajanus cajan and pods
Calophyllum inophyllum
Canarium album kernel
Canarium odontophyllum kernel
Canavalia ensiformis and pods
Canna edulis rhizome
Cargana arborescens
Carica papaya
Carum carvi
Carya spp
Caryota mitis remove poisonous fruit wall
Cassia tora
Castanea
Cercidium floridum and pods
Cercidium microphyllum
Cercis occidentalis
Chrysobalanus icaco kernel
Chrysolepis sempervirens
Cicer arietinum
Cirsium vulgare
Cola
Cordeauxia edulis
Cordia spp
Coriandrum sativum
Cucumis sativus
Corylus spp
Corypha elata and kernels
Crateva religiosa
Cucumis dipsaceus
Cucumis filcifolia
Cucumis maxima
Cucumis melo

Cucumis melo spp agrestis
Cucumis moschata
Cumimum
Cycas revoluta
Dendrocalamus strictus
Desmanthus brachylobus
Dioon edule
Durio dulcis
Emblica officinalis unripe
Eruca sativa
Erythrina edulis
Eucalyptus intertexta
Eucarya spicata
Euryale
Fagopyrum
Fagus grandifolia
Fagus sylvatica
Foeniculum dulce
Gevuina
Ginkgo biloba
Glycine max
Guizotia abyssinica
Helianthus
Helianthus annuus
Heliconia caribaea
Hertiera littoralis
Hibiscus cannabinus
Hibiscus rosa-sinensis
Hildegardia barteri
Hordeum
Impatiens glandulifera
Inga laurina
Inga paterno
Jubaea chilensis
Juglans
Kigelia africana
Lablab purpureus
Lathyrus japonicus young
pods, immature seed
Lathyrus sativus unripe seed
Lepidium sativum sprouting
Linum lewisii
Linum perenne
Lomatium macrocarpum
Luffa acutangula
Luffa cylindrica
Lupinus perennis

Macadamia
Medicago sativa sprouted
Momordica blasamina
Morinda citrifolia some forms
Moringa oleifera
Myrica rubra kernel
Myrrhis
Nelumbo lutea
Nelumbo nucifera
Nephelium lappaceum
Nicolaia elatior mature
Nuphar luteum
Nymphaea lotus
Nymphaea stellata
Nymphaea tuberosa
Nypa fruticans
Oenanthe javanica
Pachira aquatica
Pachira insignis kernel
Pandanus tectorius
Phyllostachys aurea
Pinus most spp
Pistacia
Pisum sativum
Pithecellobium dulce
Pithecellobium flexicaule
Plantago ovata sprouted
Plantago psyllium sprouted
Pleiogynium solandri
Polygonum aviculare
Pometia pinnata
Pontederia cordata
Portulaca oleracea sprouted
Proboscidea spp
Prosopis chilensis
Prosopis juliflora
Prunus americana kernel
Prunus virginiana kernel
Pterocarpus marsupium
Raphanus sativus sprouted and pod
Raphia farinifera kernel
Salacca edulis
Salicornia europaea
Salmalia malabarica
Salvia azurea v grandiflora
Salvia hispanica sprouted
Salvia viridis

Sasa kurilensis and sprouted
Scirpus validus
Sclerocarya birrea kernel
Sclerocarya caffra kernel
Scorodocarpus borneensis
Serenoa repens
Simmondsia chinensis
Sisymbrium irio
Solidago canadensis
Staphylea pinnata kernel
Sterculia spp
Tamarindus indica
Terminalia glabra
Terminalia spp kernel
Torreya californica kernel
Torreya nucifera
Trapa nutans kernel
Trifolium incarnatum sprouted
Trifolium pratense sprouted
Tropaeolum majus
Tylosema esculentum
Typha angustifolia
Vangueria infausta
Xanthoceras sorbifolium
Ximenia caffra
Yucca brevifolia
Zea mays

WARNING

Edible seeds are often only edible after some treatment. They may be poisonous if eaten raw, for instance. Never eat commercially available seed, especially vegetable seed which may have been treated with fungicides or other chemical treatments for seed sowing. This warning applies to the edible seeds above and the culinary and medicinal seeds which follow. Again, some need treatment before they are safe.IF YOU ARE UNSURE, THEN DO NOT EAT IT. The author and publisher can accept no responsibility for any mishap whatsoever occurring from misuse .

CULINARY

Seeds of grains and vegetable seed such as beans and peas offer culinary delights with which we are all familiar.

However, there are many more culinary uses of seed from condiments to coffee substitutes. Many seeds can be ground for flour or meal and many more provide us with delicious oils, such as walnut and pine kernel oil.

Abelmoschus esculentus
Abelmoschus ficulneus
Acacia aneura
Acacia giraffae
Acacia karroo
Acacia nilotica
Acacia victoriae
Acanthosicyos horridus oil
Acanthosicyos naudinanus
Acer saccharum
Achyranthes aspera
Adansonia digitata
Adansonia gregorii
Aiphanes caryotifolia
Aleurites moluccana oil
Allium sativum sprouted
Amaranthus cruentus and sprouted
Amaranthus graecizans
Amaranthus hybridus
Amaranthus hypochondriacus
Amaranthus lividus
Amaranthus mantegazzianus
Amaranthus paniculatus
Amaranthus quitoensis
Amaranthus retroflexus and sprouted
Amomum compactum
Amygdalus besseriana
Apios americana
Araucaria araucana
Arenga pinnata
Arundinaria gigantea
Atriplex some
Avena sativa
Balanties aegyptiaca

Balsamorhiza sagittata
Beninacsa
Bertholletia excelsa
Bixa orellana
Borassus aethiopum germinated seed
Brachychiton diversifolium
Brassica alba

Brassica juncea
Brassica nigra
Brosimum alicastrum
Buchanania lanzan
Calochortus nuttallii
Canarium commune
Cannabis sativa
Capsella bursa-pastoris
Caragana arborescens
Carica papaya
Carnegiea gigantea and oil
Carum carvi
Cassia floribunda
Cassia obtusifolia
Cassia occidentalis
Cassia tora
Castanea spp
Ceratotheca sesamoides
Cercidium floridum
Cercidium microphyllum
Chenopodium most spp and
some sprouted
Chrysophyllum cainito
Cicer arietinum
Cistus ladanifer
Citrullus lanatus and oil
Cleome integrifolia
Cochlospermum religiosum oil
Cocos nucifera and sprouted
Coix lacryma-jobi
Cola
Colchicum
Coriandrum sativum
Crescentia alata
Crescentia cujete
Cucumis maxima
Cucumis sativus
Cuminum cyminum and oil
Cyamopsis tetragonolobus
Dipteryx

Dolichos lignosus
Echinochloa
Elaeis guineensis oil
Elettaria cardamomum
Eleusine
Elymus canadensis
Ephedra nevadensis
Eragrostis tef
Eucalyptus microtheca
Euryale ferox
Fagopyrum
Fagus oil
Ferocactus
Foeniculum vulgare
Galium aparine
Garcinia some source of edible fat
Glyceria
Gossypium herbaceum oil
Helianthus oil
Hibiscus rosa-sinensis
Hibiscus sabdariffa
Hordeum
Hordeum vulgare
Juglans
Lagenaria siceraria
Lathyrus japonicus dried
Lathyrus sativus dried
Lens culinaris
Lepidium fremontii
Lepidium sativum
Leucaena
Levisticum
Leymus
Ligusticum scoticum
Linum usitatissimum
Lomatium macrocarpum
Luffa cylindrica oil
Lupinus albus
Lupinus luteus
Lupinus mutabilis
Macadamia
Mangifera caesia
Medicago sativa sprouted
Melilotus
Milium
Mucuna pruriens
Murraya koenigii oil

Myristica
Nigella sativa
Nuphar advena
Nuphar luteum
Nymphaea lotus
Nypa fruticans
Ocimum spp
Opuntia phaeacantha
Oroxylum indicum
Oryza
Pachycereus pecten-aboriginum
Pachycereus pringlei
Pandanus odoratissimus
Panicum miliaceum
Papaver somniferum and oil
Papver spp
Paullinia cupana
Peganum harmala
Pennisetum americanum
Perilla
Petroselinum crispum
Pettandra virginica
Phaseolus
Pimpinella anisum
Pimpinella saxifraga
Pinus spp some
Plantago lanceolata
Plantago major
Polygonum aviculare
Pontederia cordata
Prunus armeniaca oil
Prunus dulcis oil
Prunus persica oil
Punica granatum
Quercus
Raphanus sativus pods
Raphanus sativus sprouted
Robinia pseudacacia
Rumex acetosa
Rumex crispus
Salvia apiana and other spp
Salvia viridis
Sanguisorba officinalis
Sarcandra glabra
Scirpus lacustris
Secale
Sesamum indicum

Sesbania
Setaria italica
Simmondsia chinensis
Sinapsis alba sprouted
Sisymbrium altissimum
Sisymbrium officinale
Smyrnium olusatrum
Sorghum
Sporobolus
Staphylea trifolia
Stellaria media
Sterculia spp
Tamarinus indica
Theobroma cacao
Trachyspermum amni
Trapa nutans
Trigonella foenum-graecum and
sprouted
Triticum
Tropaeolum majus
Umbellularia californica
Uniola paniculata
Verbena hastata
Vicia spp
Vigna spp
Vitex negundo v cannabifolia
Washingtonia filifera
Ximenia
Yucca whipplei
Zea and oil
Zea mays
Zizania aquatica

POISONOUS SEEDS

A number of seeds are known to be poisonous and are toxic if eaten. Some toxins can be removed rendering them safe to eat. Treat all seed as unsafe unless you know them to be safe.

Poisoning has been known and deaths have occurred from eating red kidney beans which have not been boiled for ten minutes to reduce toxins before cooking for the required time.

MEDICINAL

Medicinal plants have been used for centuries. The following plants have seeds which have been or are still used medicinally in parts of the world today.

Atropa belladonna
Avena sativa
Azadirachta
Benincasa
Bixa orellana
Borago officinalis
Brucea javanica
Carica papaya
Carum carvi
Castanospermum
Citrus reticulata
Coffea arabica
Cola
Colchicum
Conium maculatum
Consolida ajacis
Coriandrum sativum
Croton
Cucumis sativus
Cuminum
Cuscuta japonica
Datura
Daucus carota
Delphinium staphisagria
Digitalis
Echinacea purpurea
Elettaria cardamomum
Eruca sativa
Euryale ferox
Fagopyrum
Fagus oil
Foeniculum
Ginkgo biloba
Gossypium herbaceum
Helianthus
Hordeum vulgare
Hydnocarpus
Leonurus sibiricus
Linum

Mucuna
Nelumbo
Nigella sativa
Nymphaea lotus
Oenothera biennis
Oryza
Papaver somniferum
Paullinia cupana
Peganum harmala
Pimpinella anisum
Plantago asatica
Psoralea corylifolia
Raphanus sativus
Salvadora persica
Salvia sclarea
Sesamum indicum
Silybum marianum
Simmondsia chinensis
Sinapsis alba
Smyrnium olusatrum
Strophanthus gratus
Strychnos nux-vomica
Thuja orientalis
Trachyspermum amni
Ziziphus jujuba

WARNING

The above seeds can only safely be used by a qualified practioner.

They are not recommended for self-treatment, and indeed some seeds such as Atropa and Strychnos are highly poisonous.

The author and publisher accept no responsibility whatsoever for any misuse of the seeds.

DECORATIVE SEEDHEADS

Leaving the seedheads on plants, not only lets the seeds dry naturally, but gives you the added bonus of attractive and decorative seedheads.

You can bring dried seedheads indoors and leave in their natural state or spray with paint. You can also dry the seedheads indoors too. You will need a light, airy place in which to hang the seedheads upside down. Rememeber to attach a paper bag to catch the seed which will inevitably fall from the pods.

Remember when you leave seed heads on the plant to dry the plant will put all its energy into producing seed, so if you want to maintain the flowering capacity of the plant, keep dead-heading and save the last seed pods when the flowers have nearly finished.

Seedheads offer a variety of shapes and sizes and are ideal for flower arranging. Some of the Australian species offer fantastic seed kernels too. Seeds themselves also have decorative uses, from poppy seed scattered onto bread to artistic uses. I have even seen greetings cards impregnated with seed.

Allium cristophii
Allium some
Alstroemeria
Alyssoides
Anemone pavoniana
Anthericum liliago
Aruncus dioicus
Asphodeline lutea
Astilbe
Cardiocrinum
Clematis
Galtonia
Gentiana lutea
Heracleum mantegazzianum
Humulus lupulus
Incarvillea delavayi
Lavatera cachemiriana
Ligularia veitchiana
Lunaria
Lysimachia ephemerum
Morina
Nigella damascena
Oxyria digyna
Papaver atlanticum
Papaver orientale
Papaver somniferum
Physalis
Physaria spp

Rheum
Sedum spectabile
Thalictrum aquilegiifolium
Typha
Valeriana alliariifolia
Veratrum nigrum

DID YOU KNOW?

There are some very interesting facts about seed. I have gathered together as many as I can to amaze and astound you.

Aeonium spectabile can only usually be raised from seed.

Agave set seed erratically in cultivation, hand-pollination can help.

Allium schoenoprasum, Chives, were used in China as long ago as 3000BC.

Allow Lathyrus odoratus seed pods to form and the plant will cease flowering, so keep picking flowers for a continuous display.

Alpine strawberries such as 'Baron Solemacher' do not produce seed and must be grown from runners.

Alstroemeria seed capsules explode.

Although Verbascum cultivars do not come true from seed, you can obtain interesting results.

Aristolochia clematitis pollination is effected by insects trapped in the hairy throat of the flower.

Artemisia abrotanum rarely flowers and sets seed except in warm climates.

Artemisia dracunculus (French Tarragon) rarely produces ripe seed in cool climates, but A. dracunculus ssp dracunculoides (Russian Tarragon) sets seed freely.

Arundo donax does not flower in the U.K.

Autumn colour is variable on seed-raised Liquidambar styracifluus.

Babiana seeds ripen to black.

Beans were used as voting tokens by the Greeks.

Berries are only produced on Skimmia spp when both sexes of the plant are grown.

Calendula seed frequently breaks into three parts either when being collected or whilst in storage, each part is viable and should not be discarded.

Canarium odontophyllum produces 70% male trees from seed.

Caraway (Carum carvi) must have full sun to produce an acceptable flavour.

Carnegiea gigantea takes 150 years to grow 12m (40ft). The first flowers appear after 40 years, setting 10 million seeds a year, but only one seedling survives in five years. Easy to germinate in cultivation.

Celmisias are usually self-sterile and only set seeds if several plants grow together.

Chicory, (Cichorium intybus) prefers a slightly alkaline soil.

Clean, plastic bags are fine for collecting, but not for storing seeds.

Convallaria majalis (Lily-of-the-Valley) rarely sets ripe seed.

Coriander (Coriandrum sativum) has been cultivated for more than 3,000 years.

Coriandrum sativum 'Morocco' is the best for seed production.

Cyclamen seed can take almost one year to ripen.

Cypripedium is extremely difficult, if not impossible to raise from seed.

Dentaria bulbifera rarely sets seed in this country.

Do not grow Dill (Anethum graveolens) and Fennel (Foeniculum vulgare) together, they cross-pollinate easily.

Double flowered cultivars of Matthiola can be selected at seedling stage at temperatures below 10°C/50°F those seedlings with yellowish green leaves will develop double flowers.

Echinopsis and Sempervivum must be hand-pollinated to set seed.

Euphorbia seed explodes when ripe.

Flowers pollinated by moths seem to rely on attracting more males than females, in some cases up to 90% and therefore males do most of the pollination.

For commercial producers kohl rabi takes 14-15 months to produce a seed crop.

Freesia do not survive if seedlings are left to dry out, or if exposed to temperatures above 10°C/50°F.

Fritillaria and Lloydia need exposure to fluctuating temperatures, keep at -2°C/28°F at night and 10°C/50°F during the day.

Glycyrrhiza glabra (Liquorice) has been used medicinally for more than 3,000 years. In cooler climates the seed is not always viable.

Good King Henry (Chenopodium bonus-henricus) has been popular since Neolithic times.

Grow Alcea as annuals or biennials to limit the risk of Hollyhock rust.

Hand-pollination is required for some species such as Holboellia latifolia to ensure fruiting.

Heat inhibits the germination of Arnica montana.

Helichrysum italicum does not normally set good seed.

If Cyclamen seed is exposed to light after soaking, it enters a second dormancy which is difficult to break.

If the seed-pods of Dictamnus are brought indoors for drying, they will explode and shoot out the seeds, then the lining of the pods will crackle.

Impatiens balsamina scatters its seed in a fit of temper.

In 1911, the branch of a female ginkgo was grafted on to the male specimen which had been planted at Kew in 1762, it took eight years to produce seed.

In general, Primula species set seed when pin-eyed and thrum-eyed plants are grown together.

Inula helenium seed is much like that of Dandelion for flying all over the garden.

Iris germanica and florentina are sterile.

It is easier to crush the entire capsule of some plants, such as Campanula medium as the seeds are so tiny and difficult to separate from the chaff.

It is said that seed from the topmost pods of Meconopsis betonicifolia produces the best plants.

It took 25 years for Cordia decandra to flower after it was planted from seed at the Veitch nursery.

It was believed that a good harvest of Parsley was only guaranteed if sown on a Good Friday.

Kalanchoe seed is sometimes very viable, at others very poor.

Laurus nobilis (Bay) sets seed in warm climates only.

Lupinus arboreus is variable from seed.

Lupinus seed strains have been developed which come true and eradicate viruses which attack old, over-propagated clones.

Lysimachia nummularia is not known to seed in the U.K.

Male and female flowers are usually borne on separate plants on Ilex spp.

Many Violas set viable seeds from insignificant greenish flowers which never open.

Mentha spp (mint) has been found in Egyptian tombs dating back to 1,000 BC.

Most autumn-sown seed germinates in spring.

Neothilic man possibly brought cornfield weeds as well as wheat seed with them when they crossed the Channel and landed in England.

Nepeta (Catmint) will germinate faster in summer.

Nerine and Amaryllis can germinate on the stem and wither and die if not collected and sown quickly.

Normally, Iris foetidissima has large pods which burst in autumn to display orange seeds, though some forms have white or yellow seeds. I. f. 'Citrina' has larger seed pods and I.f. 'Variegata' seldom flowers.

Normally the chaff needs to be removed from seed before sowing.

One of the largest seeds is that of Lodoicea, the Coco-de-Mer.

Only sow Begonia fresh if there is at least 14 hours of daylight, otherwise store at 5°C (41°F) and sow in spring.

Oxalis valdivensis has seed capsules which explode.

Pamianthe peruviana seeds take a year to ripen in capsules.

Paris polyphylla appears to be self-infertile but when two clones are grown together the resulting pods of orange-red seeds are as conspicuous as those of Iris foetidissima.

Polygonum rude has maroon seeds.

Pulmonaria officinalis (Lungwort) produces little viable seed, but does self-sow in the garden, producing variable plants.

Raise Dianthus Highland Hybrids from seed.

Ranunculus increase naturally from seed and quickly drop seed.

Records date back over 2,000 years of Sempervivum tectorum growing on the tiles of houses.

Repeated handling of the seeds of Ecballium, the squirting cucumber, may cause poisoning.

Roman legionaries brought seeds on their clothes, in the mud of horses hooves and in the fodder. Their road system spread seeds far and wide.

Roscoea 'Beesiana' is sterile.

Salvias ripen from the base and shed seeds within 2 days.

Santolina (Cotton Lavender) seed is available but is very erratic and offers poor germination.

Satureja (Savoury) has been used as a food flavouring for over 2,000 years.

Schlumbergera need to be cross-pollinated by other plants to set seed.

Seed from cultivars of Narcissus do not come true, but new cultivars are often selected from seed of crosses between cultivars, or from open-pollinated seed.

Seed of alpine Gunneras are rarely fertile.

Seed of Capsella bursa-pastoris, Shepherd's purse, were found in the stomach of Tollund man (c500BC - AD400) and during the excavation of the ancient Catal Huyuk site.

Seed of Coriandrum sativum was among the beloved items taken to America by the early settlers, and also by the Spaniards to Mexico. Seed of this species has been found in tombs from the twenty-first Egyptian dynasty (1085-945BC).

Seed of Hesperis matronalis can vary from white to deep lilac.

Seed of mature pine trees in a pine forest only travel one and a half times the height of the tree.

Seed of most species recommended to sow as soon as ripe, can also be sown in autumn, but they will not usually germinate as well.

Seed of Phlox paniculata do not normally transmit eelworm infestations.

Seed of Trapa collected in autumn need to be stored frost-free in water or wet moss over winter and sown in spring.

Seed of white plants will usually include one or two pinks, which can be discarded.

Seed of Zaluzianskya is not regularly produced in gardens.

Seed-raised plants are usually virus-free.

Seed-raised plants of Fagus sylvatica Purple Group are variable, as are those of Quercus robur f fastigiata and Betula.

Seedling nut trees are not reliably fruitful, just as seedling apples are not the same as grafted apple trees.

Seeds of Nigella sativa were used in the sixteenth century as a relish and stimulant for the taste buds.

Self-fertile seeds of Mammillaria often set seed, taking up to one year to form candle like pods.

Smaller seedlings of Petunia and Matthiola, for example, usually give the best colour.

Some Lilium spp such as L .auratum, L. candidum, L. henryi, L. japonicum and L. martagon germinate quickly from fresh seed, but the leaves do not appear until the following growing season, Keep pots moist and shaded for at least two years.

Sow seed of short-lived perennials such as Linaria alpina and Viola frequently to keep a constant supply.

Spores of the widely distributed Cyrtomium falcatum would be best obtained from the colder districts of Japan for British gardens.

Stored Colchicum seed may not germinate for up to four years, whereas fresh seed germinates readily.

Stratiodes aloides rarely forms seed in cold climates, including the U.K.

Syringa vulgaris are variable in flower colour from seed.

Tanacetum balsamita grown in cool climates will not produce viable seed.

Taraxacum officinale (Dandelion) was used medicinally by the Arabs in the 11th century.

Tecophilaeas rarely set seed in cooler climates, so hand-pollinate.

Telopea truncata f lutea is an unusual form with yellow flowers. However, when seed-raised it will mostly bear red flowers due to open-pollination.

Temperatures over 24°C(84°F) inhibit germination of Rebutia.

Thalictrum delavayi 'Hewitts' Double' is sterile and therefore can only be increased by division.

The best flower spikes on Cardiocrinum occur on bulbs raised from seed.

The black seeds amongst the brightly coloured ones in pods of Paeonia are the fertile ones.

The capsules of Celastrus spp split open in autumn to reveal a yellow lining of colourful red seeds.

The cones of Pinus muricata have been known to remain intact for 30 to 40 years, the seeds eventually being liberated by forest fires.

The erect, woody cones of Widdringtonia remain for some time after shedding seed.

The flesh of the berries of Arisaema may inhibit germination.

The fruits of Juniperus horizontalis are rarely produced in cultivation.

The fruits of Viburnum farreri are rare in cultivation.

The immense white blooms of Hymenocallis macrostephana turn reddish after pollination.

The juice of Arum berries is caustic, so wear gloves.

The seed heads of Impatiens split apart and coil backwards so suddenly when ripe that the seeds are ejected several feet from the plant.

The seed heads of Nymphaea sink as seeds ripen.

The seed of Levisticum, lovage was chewed by the Greeks to aid digestion and relieve flatulence.

The seed of Talinum okanoganense falls very quickly from the pod.

The seed pods of Iris pseudacorus

'Bastardii' and a variegated form should be picked to avoid reversion.

The seed-heads of Ozothamnus ledifolius emit a sweet, honey-like aroma.

The seeds in the opening pods of Paeonia are highly-coloured cerise and blue or scarlet and black, in many species and varieties. Those of P. obovata alba are brilliant blue and those of P.veitchii are bluish.

The seeds of Celastrus orbiculatus split to reveal bright yellow insides.

The seeds of Corydalis flexuosa need to be collected when still green as they fall before they are ripe.

The seeds of Gentiana kurroo are usually reluctant to germinate.

The seeds of Geranium maderense will still disperse like a self-detonating mechanism, even after picked.

The seeds of the true Aquilegia glandulosa are dull, not shiny and glossy like other Aquilegias.

The sexes of Erodium chrysanthum are carried on separate plants, the plant bearing male flowers being less beautiful than the female, if seed is desired both plants must be present.

There are more than 250 species of Aloe.

There are more than 750 species of Salvia, Sage.

Tricyrtis seed develops late in the season and is therefore not always available in colder climates.

Veratrum species are very slow from seed.

When growing from seed, always select the best coloured forms for purple plants or variegated forms.

When Magnolia campbellii is raised from seed the flowers are usually pink, but may vary between white and deep rose-purple. The deeper coloured forms are usually the least hardy.

X Zenobia pulverulenta f nitida said to occur in the wild and is regarded by some as a distinct species. Seed-grown plants in cultivation contain forms which appear to be intermediate between the two.

Yucca species do not set seed in the U.K.

YEAR ROUND SEEDS

Whenever seeds are featured in magazines or on radio or television, it always seems to be in spring, yet seeds can be sown almost all year round. So, instead of being rushed in spring, you can sow all year.

Of course this depends on what you want to sow. Most annuals will be sown in spring but they can be sown again in early autumn for winter pots indoors and for early flowers the next spring. Do not confine your seed sowing just to spring, plan year-round sowings, although winter will be your quietest time. I have divided the following easy-access table into the seasons and listed what can be sown.

Spring
Annuals direct
Annuals under cover
Biennials
Perennials, including some which can be sown as annuals
Herbs under cover
Shrubs
Climbers
Vegetables
Grasses
Conifers
Trees
Bulbs

Summer
Annuals direct
Biennials
Vegetables
Some sow as soon as ripe species

Autumn
Annuals for winter pots or early spring flowers
Grasses
Perennials in cold frames
Trees in cold frames
Trees in seedbed
Vegetables to overwinter
Soon as ripe species

Winter (late)
Tender perennials under cover which require a slightly longer growing season.
Tender bulbs such as Freesia.
Vegetables under cover

SEED COLLECTING

VEGETABLES

Collecting seed of vegetables is usually worthwhile if they are not F1's which will not come true. Many organisations exist around the world to save seed of heirloom and traditional varieties.

To save seed from your garden you need to observe the distances as cross-pollination will occur with other varieties of the same species or with other crops . For example, Beetroot will cross with Chard and Broccoli will cross with other members of the Cabbage family, so you will need to keep these plants separated if you wish to save seed. For other crops such as Brussel sprouts you will need more than one plant to save seed. Recommended distances vary from country to country and are higher for certified seed.

Distance

Amaranth 400 metres
Aubergine 400 metres
Carrot 500 metres
Cauliflower at least 500 metres
Chicory 400 metres
Chinese cabbage 400 metres
Corn at least 500 metres
Cucumber 500 metres
Fennel 400 metres
Melon 400 metres
Okra 30 metres
Onion 400 metres
Pepper 200 metres
Watermelon 400 metres
Welsh onion 100 metres

THE EASIEST CROPS

Some crops are easier than others for seed saving, so if you are a beginner, start with some of the crops below.
Broad bean
Fennel
French bean
Garlic
Lettuce
Pea
Tomato

Beans of all types are easy to keep pure and are a favourite crop of seed savers.

A good lettuce can produce 60,000 seeds from one plant.

It is difficult to keep corn strains pure.

Crops can be caged or separeted by a taller crop with which it does not cross-pollinate.

Pumpkin, marrow and squash are better hand-pollinated.

TOMATO SEEDS

Allow the fruits to ripen just beyond the eating stage. Cut in half and squeeze the seed into a bowl. Label and leave for 2-3 days. Do not disturb and do not leave for more than 4 days. This allows a thick skin to form. Scoop the skin off and rinse the seed thoroughly in a metal sieve under running water. Dry the seeds on kitchen paper. They can be placed in a labelled envelope and hung up to dry for 2 weeks. Store in a cool, dry place for up to 4 years.

SOWING A LAWN

Lawns are still very popular in the U.K but less so where they are subject to periods of very dry weather. There is a trend for people to dispense with the lawn and cover the area with other plants or gravel.

Lawn seed mixtures vary and you can choose the right mix for a hard-wearing or ornamental lawn, sun or shade. A lawn once there usually stays put, so make sure you prepare the ground well for sowing. Lawns are usually sown in early autumn or spring. Start your preparations well in advance.

Preparing the site

1. Remove any stones, lumps and weeds. Dig over and level the area. Incorporate well-rotted organic matter to a depth of 25cm (10in). Perennial weeds such as dandelion need to be eradicated, spot treat. Improve heavy, clay soils with gravel or drainage pipes if necessary.
2. A few days before sowing, firm the soil by treading or using a roller. Rake to a fine tilth. Sow after rainfall or irrigate the site.
3. Sow with a machine for large areas or by hand. Mark out the area into sections of equal size. Weigh out enough seeds for one section. Scatter half the seeds across and half down the area. Seeds can be mixed with sand for even distribution.
4. Cover if the site is of a practical size to protect from birds. Remove as soon as germination occurs. This usually takes 7-10 days.

SPROUTING SEEDS

Many of the seeds in the edible and culinary uses section can be sprouted. Prepared in this way, the seeds are highly nutritious, protein and vitamin levels being at their highest.

Always use untreated seed and only seed you know is safe to eat. The time it takes for seeds to sprout varies from 3-10 days. You can sprout many small beans such as Aduki and Mung, you can also sprout Alfalfa (Medicago) and Fenugreek amongst others.

In a jar

1. Sterilize a jam-jar. Place a small amount of seeds in the jar in 2.5cm (1in) of cold water. Cover with muslin and seal with a rubber band, drain off the water.
2. Leave in a warm place, dark place at 21°C (70°F).
3. Rinse twice daily until sprouted.

In a tray

1. Line a seed tray with moistened blotting paper or kitchen towel.
2. Place the seeds in the tray.
3. Keep the seeds at 21°C (70°F).

GLOSSARY

Some of the horticultural terms which occur in the book are explained below.

Acid soil
With a pH value below 7.

Aeration
Opening up of soil structure allowing free circulation of air.

Angiosperm
Flowering plant that bears ovules, later seeds, enclosed in an ovary.

Bisexual
Flowers bearing male and female reproductive organs.

Chromosome
String of genes contained within a cell nucleus. Transmit hereditary characteristics.

Cotyledon
The first set of leaves produced by the germinating seed and known as seed leaves.

Dioecious
Male and female flowers are borne on separate plants, both being necessary for the formation of fruit.

Drill
A narrow, straight furrow in the soil into which seeds can be sown.

F1 Hybrids
Uniform, vigorous offspring resulting from controlled crosses.

Gymnosperm
Tree or shrub, usually evergreen, that bears naked seeds in cones rather than in enclosed ovaries.

Hybrid
The offspring of genetically different parents.

Monocarpic
Plants which flower once then die.

Monoecious
Having separate male and female flowers on the same plant.

Open-pollinated
Varieties which result from natural pollination.

Parent Plant
A plant providing seeds or other material for propagation. Sometimes known as the mother plant.

Self-fertile
A plant that produces viable seeds when fertilized with its own pollen.

Self-pollination
The transfer of pollen from one flower to the same or other flowers on the same plant.

Self-seed
A plant which seeds itself with no help.

Self-sterile
A plant needing pollen from another individual of the species to produce seeds.

A comprehensive horticultural dictionary is included in Plant Names A-Z, see inside back cover.

DISCLAIMER

Although there are uses given for seeds in this book, including edible seed and culinary and medicinal uses, this in no way guarantees nor indicates that these seeds are safe. Do not attempt to treat yourself with any seeds, nor to eat seed unless you are sure it is safe. The information given is general and is primarily included out of interest to the reader.

INDEX